SPOKEN from the HEART

Volume 2

SPOKEN
from the HEART

Volume 2

FURTHER POWERFUL TALKS AND ADDRESSES
THAT HAVE BLESSED AND INSPIRED

BY

SELWYN HUGHES

Published 2006 by CWR, Waverley Abbey House, Waverley Lane, Farnham, Surrey GU9 8EP, UK.

See back of book for list of National Distributors.

Concept development, editing, design and production by CWR
Cover image: Jeffery Howe, Roger Walker

Printed in Finland by WS Bookwell

ISBN-13: 978-1-85345-403-5
ISBN-10: 1-85345-403-6

~ CONTENTS ~

~ FOREWORD ~

Selwyn Hughes was undoubtedly one of the finest popular preachers of his generation. As someone privileged to work alongside him in the later years of his ministry, I can bear witness to this. I can picture him now, on our last overseas ministry trip together, sitting with his leg propped up on a stool to offset the pain, caused by his bone cancer, holding an audience of three thousand spellbound – and this in a marriage seminar! He had the evangelist's love of a crowd but the counsellor's skill of seeming to address each individual in it at a deeply personal level.

We talked once about a long-forgotten book on preaching by the nineteenth-century Congregational divine, Sylvester Horne, called *The Romance of Preaching*. Neither of us could remember anything about the book except its title which attracted and intrigued us.

Selwyn was a 'romantic' about preaching. He was passionately committed to it as God's chief means of grace to convert sinners and build up believers. That the Bible 'speaks today' and 'speaks' with authority, was for him a settled conviction. In a day when biblical preaching is increasingly being disparaged within the Church, he gave enormous encouragement to countless would-be and practising preachers to stay faithful to their calling. And he urged them to develop their gift. Like his main mentor, W.E. Sangster, he saw preaching as an art or a craft. To that end he loved words, caressing and polishing them as you might precious jewels. He would employ any stratagem, commandeer any story, harness any humour, as long as it all served his passionate purpose of 'saving souls' and 'sanctifying saints' – as he might have phrased it. Nothing was too much trouble – whether care in choosing the apt quotation, or setting up the lectern, or tinkering with the public address system – as long as it enabled him better to get his message across.

He rarely went deep *into* a text. Rather, like the Welsh Rugby fly-half he might have been, he picks up the text and sets off with it on a jinking run, darting and weaving past our mental and spiritual defences, until joyfully he grounds the truth in the human heart.

He stayed wryly detached from mood swings in the Church. Unashamedly, he remained a successful rhetorician long after critics decried such a skill. He was a marvellous storyteller long before it came into fashion. Was he occasionally over-fond of allegorising (as in 'The Four Anchors')? Perhaps, but then, no less a preaching luminary as James S. Stewart did the same and with the same text. As a herald of the gospel of grace, his over-riding concern was to apply this gospel transformingly to the human condition, and in this he invariably succeeded.

It may seem odd to compare so essentially private and reserved a man as Selwyn with John the Baptist. But like the Baptist, he consecrated all his energy and gifts to point his listeners to the Lamb of God. Having been blessed of God with signs and wonders in his early evangelistic ministry, Selwyn in later years devoted himself to prayer and the ministry of the Word. What was said about John could be said of Selwyn in his final years, that though he performed no miraculous signs, 'everything he said about Jesus was true' – and that is wonder enough!

Like John the Baptist, he endeavoured to be the best man to the Bridegroom. Believing in the romance of preaching, he devoted all his considerable skills to being the matchmaker between Jesus and the human heart. Like John the Baptist, Selwyn gave his life to be a spokesman for the Word, a mouthpiece for His Master's Voice.

I warmly commend these printed sermons to you as a further sample of Selwyn's legacy. Listen to them prayerfully and you will surely hear that Voice for yourself.

Philip Greenslade,
Waverley Abbey House, autumn 2006.

1

THE PUNCTUALITY OF GOD

GALATIANS 4:4; ROMANS 5:6; ACTS 2:1; MATTHEW 25:13; 2 CORINTHIANS 6:2

When I was preparing for the ministry I was told that a good preacher needs only one text, a moderately good preacher needs two and a bad preacher will need three or more. Well, I have five for you!

The longer I live and the more I study the Scriptures, the more convinced I am that somewhere at the back of the universe God has a clock that keeps perfect time. He runs the world by the tick of its pendulum. Down through the running ages God has never been a moment too soon, or a moment too late. He is always on time. I am speaking metaphorically, of course, because God does not have a literal clock. I am using the term to describe the fact that everything God does is according to a controlling schedule: the ocean tides ebb and flow – right on time; the stars come out at night – right on time; the flowers flame forth in spring – right on time; the sun rises and sets – right on time.

You can see this attention to timekeeping not only in nature but in the life of men and women, for there is, according to Ecclesiastes, a time to be born and a time to die. The whole universe appears to be working to a divine timetable and it is the supreme paradox of history that whilst God is eternal He is always on time – never too early or too late.

But it is particularly in relation to the great question of our salvation that this feature of the divine character comes out most markedly. It is in this connection that we best behold the amazing timekeeping of God.

My first text is Galatians 4:4:

But when the time had fully come, God sent his Son, born of a woman, born under law, to redeem those under law, that we might receive the full rights of sons.

The coming of Christ to Bethlehem was neither late nor early, neither behind nor beforehand, neither tardy nor premature. Charles Wesley's carol, *Hark the Herald Angels Sing*, says: 'Late in time, behold Him come ...' As a boy, whenever I sang that carol, I used to ponder how it was possible to be both things at once, late and in time, wondering if I could achieve the same feat in relation to my school attendance. But Jesus was not late. Although it might have appeared that He was late, He came at the divinely appointed hour. His advent chimed exactly with the striking of the great clock of God. Make no mistake about it, His birth was not a last minute brainstorm by the Creator, some hectic attempt to rescue mankind. God had prepared this even before the foundation of the world. He announced His coming way back in time. He predicted it through prophecy. People get some predictions wrong. We can't predict the weather exactly, for example. But there are hundreds of prophecies about Jesus' coming: Genesis 3:15 was the first prophecy of Scripture, Micah 5:2 speaks prophetically of Bethlehem as His birthplace, Isaiah 7:14 says He will be born of a virgin and Hosea 11:1 refers to the time when the family of Jesus would take refuge in Egypt. It was no fluke that Jesus arrived when He did.

Must not His coming have seemed strangely delayed to the Old Testament saints? How wistfully they waited for the fulfilment of the prophetic promises. How piously and prayerfully they hoped for the emergence of the Messiah. During His lifetime, the Messiah turned to His disciples one day, saying: 'For I tell you that many prophets and kings wanted to see what you see but did not see it, and to hear what you hear but did not hear it' (Luke 10:24).

'When will our Messiah come?' cried the great prophets of the Old Testament. But the centuries rolled by and there was no answer. He did not come. 'Give us a Christ!' the world was saying in effect. But He did not come. Then one day, God's clock struck the right hour and He came down the stairs of eternity with a baby in His arms.

Why did God come in the form of a baby? Because He did not come to scare us, but to save us. Many people are afraid of God. They don't even like to talk about Him – it makes them nervous. If I were God I would have lit up the heavens and shaken the earth to get people's attention. But it would have been frightening if God had come in thunder and put on a giant light show. Who is afraid of a baby? The Word became flesh and a little bundle of life moved in a crib at Bethlehem – the greatest mystery. God became a baby. Wow! What a baby! When we peer by imagination into the face of the baby in Bethlehem, we can say, as we can of no other in history, 'Now that is some baby!' He is the only baby who ever lived before He was conceived!

Jesus' birth is the most significant event in history. That's why we celebrate it. In fact, all of history is split in half by this one event. It's a big deal! He is the reference point for every date in history because He was that important. Every time we write the date, who are we using as a reference point? Christ and His birth. Even atheists unwittingly refer to Him each time they use the date! That's how important His birth is. God came to earth in the form of a baby.

Now I believe a good case could be made out for the contention that Jesus should have come earlier than He did, that He came too late. Think of the joy if His advent had happened hundreds of years before it did. What would it have done to men like Job and David and Isaiah and Jeremiah? Yet He did not arrive on the scene in the life of those great figures of biblical history. As the New Testament writer to the Hebrews put it: 'These were all commended for their faith, yet none of them received what had been promised' (Heb. 11:39).

On the other hand, there have been those who have not hesitated to declare that Christ came not too late but too early, that He was ahead of time not behind it. Would it not have been better if He had delayed His coming until now and taken advantage of our printing, Internet, photographs, tapes, CNN, Sky news and so on? When I was in the Holy Land a few years ago, I saw a television station just above the hill of Nazareth and I thought, if Jesus arrived today He would be able to blaze the message of the gospel around the world! When we think of that – and the joy of His coming now – are we not half inclined to say, 'Yes, perhaps He came too early'?

Paul will have nothing to do with either of these arguments: 'But when the time had fully come,' he says, 'God sent his Son.' At the right time.

Why did God choose this time in the history of the world to send His Son? Let me see if I can give some insight into this.

IT WAS THE RIGHT TIME CULTURALLY

The stage had been set for Christ's coming as, 350 years before He came, the son of the Macedonian king, Philip II, was born, whom we know as Alexander the Great. He conquered the world and brought tremendous changes to what we now know as Europe and the Middle

East. Greek culture – embracing philosophy, the arts, drama, literature, architecture and thought – all took a leap forward under him and broke down barriers of nationalism. Travelling people shared concepts, and the Greek language became a language that united the world. It was a second language to most people and became the language of commerce. In 280 BC the Jewish Scriptures began to be translated into Greek and became known as the Septuagint.

IT WAS THE RIGHT TIME POLITICALLY

The Romans had by then taken over the divided and declining territories that Alexander had conquered and had imposed the famous Pax Romana, which meant, in effect, 'enforced peace'. Woe betide you if you stepped out of line: you would feel the iron fist of Roman imperialism! They crisscrossed the lands they ruled with paved roads, creating a network that we still benefit from and giving rise to the saying 'all roads lead to Rome'. They also established an efficient postal system.

God even had a hand in those who would ascend to power. Caesar Augustus was in power at the time Jesus was born, and little did he know when he called for a census that he was, in fact, doing God's will. The edict that all people return to their place of origin to be counted, meant a pregnant Mary with her husband Joseph made the historic journey to Bethlehem. She was guided by the sovereignty of God to the place where Jesus was to be born, as prophesied in the Old Testament.

IT WAS THE RIGHT TIME SPIRITUALLY

God gave us the Law not to make us better but to reveal to us the state of our hearts. It was a mirror or, by another analogy, our schoolmaster to bring us to Christ. When you compare yourself to some people you feel good, but when you compare yourself to the Law you see the truth.

The Law makes us conscious of our sin.

The Jews were ready. The Law had served its purpose – done its time, so to speak. The world now had a clear picture, as if taken by X-ray, of the depraved human heart and could recognise that 'it's all in here'. Jesus came to live under the Law and to experience it. There had been 400 years of silence. The Law had done its very educational work. It had shown through the Jewish nation what we humans are like, that we are transgressors. The world was spiritually starved and the worship of false gods had left many people spiritually empty and barren.

The Greeks had created unity of language, the Romans had prepared the roads, the Hebrews had kept alive the Scriptures. All three coalesced, making this the first time in history when everything was perfect for Jesus' arrival and for the gospel to be carried to all parts of the Roman Empire.

God had two plans for our salvation. Plan A and Plan B. There are two ways to get to heaven. One of them is to be perfect: never sin, never think a bad thought, never do a bad thing; always be unselfish and never hurt anyone. If you were to appear before God and He were to ask, 'Why should I let you into heaven – this is a perfect place?', you could say, 'Because I am perfect', and He would let you in. 'Right, come on in,' He would say.

But Plan A got messed up. Since the Fall, no one is perfect. Not one of us can claim to be without sin. If I could put up a screen and project onto it all the thoughts you have ever had, you would be embarrassed and ashamed. That goes for me too. We all live with a sense of regret, for no one is perfect. That's why we need a Saviour.

So God came up with Plan B. He said, 'I will send to earth My Son who will live a perfect life'. That Son died for our imperfections and His perfection was credited to our account. So now, when I get to heaven, if

God says, 'Why should I let you in, Selwyn?' I'm not going to say, 'Because I'm perfect', but, 'Because I have put my trust in Jesus who said, "Come to me and I will give you life."' And God is going to say, 'Come on in!'

God's Plan B was to redeem those under the Law so that we might receive *the adoption of sons.* Adoption is a beautiful concept! God's Plan A was that everyone, being perfect, should come to Him. His Plan B is that we can come in *His strength and power.*

And so to Bethlehem He came as our Saviour – *at the right time!*

The timing of God is seen everywhere in Scripture. It's a favourite theme of mine. Not only did Jesus come to Bethlehem on time, but He went to the cross on time also.

And this brings us to my second text:

You see, at just the right time, when we were still powerless, Christ died for the ungodly.

Rom. 5:6

Jesus revealed Himself in Scripture as a Man with a mission, moving towards a predetermined hour and, as He moved through the world, He seemed to have His eye on an unseen clock. At the very start of His ministry Jesus was a guest at a wedding feast in Cana when, disastrously, the wine ran out. His mother reported this fact to Jesus, obviously expecting that He would seize upon this as a moment of glory, an opportunity to make Himself known. But His reply to her was, 'Dear woman, why do you involve me? ... My time has not yet come' (John 2:4). On several other occasions, it is reported in Scripture, He declared His time had 'not yet come'. Then there came a time when, as it is told in John 17:1, '... Jesus ... looked towards heaven, and prayed: "Father, the time has come. Glorify your Son, that your Son may glorify you.'

He came right on time at Pentecost too, which leads us to my third text:

> When the Day of Pentecost came, they were all together in one place.
>
> Acts 2:1

When Jesus went away from this world to take His place at the right hand of His Father, He told His disciples not to leave Jerusalem but to wait there for the gift His Father had promised – baptism with the Holy Spirit. And there they waited – praying in the upper room – a group of 120 disciples, including the women, Mary the mother of Jesus and his brothers. But nothing happened, day after day, until the tenth day when suddenly the Holy Spirit arrived. He came with a sound like the blowing of a violent wind, appearing in the form of tongues of fire that separated and came to rest on each of the disciples. And we know what occurred next: 'All of them were filled with the Holy Spirit and began to speak in other tongues as the Spirit enabled them' (2:4). Why can we say that He arrived at just the right time? Why was the timing of this event so crucial? Because the tenth day coincided with the Feast of Pentecost, when crowds would be jostling in the streets and filling the Temple. With all this going on in Jerusalem, it was just the right moment for the Holy Spirit to come!

What a difference the coming of the Holy Spirit made to their lives and what a difference He makes when He comes in these days into our lives.

I gave my life to Jesus Christ when I was sixteen years of age and the shyest person you could ever meet. God said to me, 'I am calling you into the ministry,' and I said, 'Lord, I will do anything for You provided You don't ask me to speak to a group of people.' And I have spent the rest of my life doing just that! Because of my shyness and timidity, my fears and apprehensions, I knew that if I were to do the work of God I needed His power from on high. I had turned to Christ and I knew that Jesus was living in my heart by His Spirit but, one Saturday night I went to a church and I heard a preacher talk about the Holy Spirit in such a way that I knew I had to ask for that divine power of which Scripture speaks. I knelt down and the Holy Spirit came into my life, filled me with power and transformed me in a moment of time. The following morning (it was a Sunday), at about nine o'clock, I stood out in the street of the little village where I lived, a sleepy little village of about five or six hundred people, with the houses all joined together in terraced rows. There was not a sound to be heard except the barking of dogs and the bells of the boys on their bicycles delivering the newspapers, and, at the top of my voice I shouted, 'For God so loved the world that he gave his one and only Son, that whoever believes in him shall not perish but have eternal life.' All the doors began to open and people came out in their pyjamas, rubbing their eyes, to see what was going on. I had the joy of preaching my very first sermon, which lasted about three minutes, right there on the street! And all that happened because of the power of the Holy Spirit. He came at just the right time into my life.

And now let's consider my fourth text:

Watch therefore, for you know neither the day nor the hour in which the Son of Man is coming.

Matt. 25:13, NKJV

No one knows the exact day when Jesus will come again but we can be sure that He will come – right on time! There is a day coming when Jesus will return, bringing the end of the age. It is not only Christians who are talking about the end of the age; there are scientists and politicians who anticipate a time when, because of the destructive power we have amassed, the world will be blown to smithereens. Such an event has seemed imminent at particular times in recent history, but political developments have so far averted it. However, there is a sense in the world, causing gloom and despondency and hopelessness, of a clock that keeps ticking, bringing the end of the age ever nearer. The fact is that the end of the age is preordained by God. Scripture teaches clearly that Jesus Christ will return, and this second coming of Jesus is referred to no less than 300 times in the New Testament. We affirm our belief in this every time we recite the creeds in our church services: '... he is seated at the right hand of the Father and *he will come* to judge both the living and the dead' (emphasis added). There is no hope for anyone except in Jesus Christ.

And now here is my fifth text:

> For he says: 'In an acceptable time I have heard you, And in the day of salvation I have helped you.' Behold, now is the accepted time; behold, now is the day of salvation.
>
> 2 Cor. 6:2, NKJV

Not only did Christ come at the right time to Bethlehem, not only did He come at the right time to Calvary, not only did He arrive at Pentecost right on time, not only will He come again right on time to bring the age to an end, but there is a time when He wants to meet with every one of us. He has appointed that time, and that time for you is *right now*. Hebrews 3:15 says, 'Today, if you hear his voice, do not harden your hearts as you did in the rebellion.'

The Bible always emphasises the fact that when we meet with God we can be absolutely certain that we don't arrive late in His presence, that we can stand before Him and say, 'Lord, I hear Your voice. You're calling me now, and this is the moment of my response.'

When I was a pastor in Yorkshire many years ago, in the 1950s and early 60s, I remember a student coming to me one day. He was a young man of about nineteen or twenty, just about to go to university, and we talked about the need for Him to receive Jesus Christ as His Saviour and Lord. He said to me, 'Selwyn, I would like to receive Jesus Christ but I want to go to university and study and get my degree and perhaps, in about a year's time, I will come back and then I will surrender my life to Jesus Christ.' And I said, 'You're living dangerously. I can promise you right now, at this moment, that if you give your life to Jesus Christ He will receive you and save you. I can guarantee that right now. But one year from now, I can't guarantee that you will be alive.' I didn't know it at that time, but I was speaking prophetically, because nine months later that young man got into a car and one of the car's tyres blew and he crashed into a telegraph post and was instantly killed. Now, wouldn't you think if somebody said, 'Lord, I'll come back in a year's time and give my life to you,' that God could stretch His grace? Wouldn't you think that He would just hold off? But, you see, there is no way that we can guarantee the future. What we can guarantee is what happens right now. Now is the accepted time. *Today*, if you hear His voice, harden not your hearts.

Let me tell you now about two girls I knew who were in my church, but not Christians. They came to an evangelistic crusade that we were holding in the church, and night after night young people came to know

Jesus Christ. But these two young girls said, 'No, we'll go away and think it over. We're going away for a holiday to the north of Scotland for three weeks and we'll talk about it and then we'll come back and we'll give our lives to Jesus Christ.' They went away on holiday, and one day they went swimming in one of the Scottish lochs, got caught in some reeds and both were drowned. Wouldn't you think that God could have stretched a point for three weeks? But the Bible teaches that we can be sure of meeting God today. That's what God's Word says. However, it doesn't teach that meeting God tomorrow can be guaranteed. No preacher of the gospel has any authority to say, 'Think it over. Come back next week and then decide for Christ.'

D.L. Moody was a great American preacher and the pastor of a church in Chicago now called Moody Memorial Church. That man went to his grave with a sad spirit because one night he got up in his pulpit and preached on the text: 'What shall I do then with Jesus which is called Christ?' (Matt. 27:22, AV). It was a marvellous message and there were thousands of people in the auditorium, but he finished his message in an unusual way. His usual way was to give an invitation after every message, but this night he stood up and said, 'Now I want to ask you, "What will you do with Jesus, which is called Christ?" And I want you to go out tonight and next Sunday night I want you to come back and answer that question, "What will you do with Jesus, which is called Christ?"' But that congregation never came back because the following day the great fire of Chicago swept through the city and many of those people who were in the church that night were killed in the fire.

A week? Why can't God stretch His grace for a week? Ah, this is a mystery that I cannot fathom and that's why I have to stand solidly as a preacher of the gospel and say this: 'I cannot promise you tomorrow, but I can promise you today.' Today if you hear His voice, do not harden your hearts. 'Now is the accepted time', says the scripture.

When I started as a young evangelist many years ago, I can remember going to a little Welsh mining village. I had one of my first evangelistic crusades in a very small church in the centre of the village and I remember praying very much at that time that God would move the whole area. Night after night many young people came into the church and among them I spotted one fine-looking young girl, and I said to myself, 'Oh, I would love to win her for Jesus Christ!' I spoke to her every night asking, 'When are you going to give your life to Christ?' 'Maybe tomorrow', she would say – and the same thing happened time after time.

We started the crusade on a Sunday night and, when we got to Thursday night, I remember standing at the door of the church and pleading with her, 'Why don't you give your heart to Jesus tonight?' 'I'll tell you what', she said, 'tomorrow night I'll come back and do it'. The girl went home that night, went to bed and awoke about three o'clock in the morning with stomach trouble. She told her mother, 'I can't sleep. I feel so ill. I don't know what's wrong with me. I feel terrible. Some strange words are going around in my mind – Ezekiel 7:3. Ezekiel 7:3'. Her mother said, 'Why, Ezekiel is a book of the Bible. Let me go and see what it says'. Together they sat at the table and her mother opened up the book of Ezekiel to the place and read these words: 'Now is the end come upon thee ... and [I] will judge thee according to thy ways' (AV). And that young girl fell across the table, dead. I conducted her funeral and I didn't know what to say. But the news spread all through the locality. We had miners coming from the pits into the church, even before they had washed their faces, to give their lives to Jesus Christ. I have never been closer to revival in the whole of my life than in those two weeks. That whole community was transformed because they realised that God was at work there.

God forbid that I should try to frighten anybody into salvation, but I have a responsibility to tell you that God has a time for you to be saved and that time is now. Right now you have an appointment with destiny and the clock of God is striking out the hour. At this moment God is coming to you and inviting you to receive Him into your life. You may belong to a church, but perhaps you have never had a personal encounter with Jesus Christ. You've never had your sins forgiven and you're not sure that you're a Christian. God says, 'Now is the accepted time ... Today if you hear my voice harden not your hearts.' This is the moment of destiny for you, a time to ask what you are doing with your life. Jesus Christ is wanting to speak to you, to save you and give you the gift of eternal life, to cleanse away every single sin you've ever committed, to change your life and make you a changed person by the power of God and the grace of His Holy Spirit.

God is saying, 'Now is the time to surrender your life to me. Give me the whole of your life and I'll meet with you.' If it is healing that you need, He can heal you. If you have wandered away from God and His grace, if once you were a fiery, burning Christian but now the fire has died low and there is no glow in your experience, then God can set your life alight once again as you surrender your whole being to Him. God's clock is striking in heaven and He is right on time for His appointment to meet with you. *Don't you be late!*

2

BE KIND TO
ONE ANOTHER

EPHESIANS 4:32

And be kind to one another, tenderhearted, forgiving one another, even as God in Christ forgave you. (NKJV)

This is a verse I repeat to myself almost every day. Apart from its spiritual truth, I love the sheer cadence and rhythm of its language. I have loved words ever since I came across them. They fascinate me. Words are the tools of my trade. Some work with figures; I work with words. Sometimes, when I am writing, I will spend five minutes searching for the right word as opposed to the almost right word. And there are times when just changing words around in a sentence makes a difference to its impact on the mind. I challenge anyone to improve on this sentence from Scripture. I regard it as a perfect piece of prose. And within it I hear the sweetest possible music – the music of the grace of God.

The verse is made even more beautiful by comparing it to the preceding verse which says: 'Let all bitterness, wrath, anger, clamour, and evil speaking be put away from you, with all malice' (v.31, NKJV). Now every one of those words is ugly. Put together, they remind you of a dull November day in Britain when the dark clouds roll up over the sky, hiding the face of the sun and shutting off its warmth, causing the heart to shiver. But then, in the next verse (the verse I have taken as my text), it is as if the sun breaks through and sheds its warmth and light and the heart is cheered once again. Listen to it once more: '... *be kind to one another, tenderhearted, forgiving one another, even as God in*

Christ forgave you.' What a wonderful contrast! God be praised!

Let me break open the text phrase by phrase. Take the words *'be kind to one another'*.

However we look at it, this is a clear command of God. If we are Christians then kindness is not optional. We are expected to be kind. It's part of the Christian lifestyle. To be a Christian and not to be kind is an absurd contradiction. But, when you think about it, it's a sad fact that we ever have to be reminded of the need to be kind. The benefits of being kind are so positive in themselves that we ought not to need a command like this. But let me name a few of the benefits.

FIRSTLY, WE WILL NEVER REGRET BEING KIND

How many of us carry regrets in our hearts concerning the past? I know I do. Things I wish had never happened. Often I think to myself as I look back on my life: I wish I had never done that ... I wish I had never said that. The interesting thing is that almost all my regrets in life are the things I have said or done that can be labelled unkind. I have regretted being unkind but I have never regretted being kind.

I have met many people in my life whose souls are torn with regrets for the things they have done in the past. The most troubled, I have found, are older men who regret being unkind to their wives. I carry a picture in my mind from the days when I was a pastor and visited an old man who was very ill. I remember how, as we talked, whenever his wife came into the room his eyes followed her everywhere she went. Later he burst out with, 'Oh God, what have I done to that woman? I have been so unkind to her throughout our life together.'

His eyes filled with tears. I knew something of their domestic circumstances and said, 'But I know she has forgiven you for that – and so also has God.'

'I know', he said, 'but how I wish I had never been so mean and hurtful'.

Despite all my attempts to help him he died a sad and unhappy man.

No, take it from me you will never regret being kind.

SECONDLY, AN ACT OF KINDNESS LIVES ON IN ONE'S MEMORY, SOMETIMES FOR A LIFETIME

Paul, looking back upon the experience of the shipwreck that brought him to Malta, remembered one thing above all others. He said, 'the ... people showed us unusual kindness' (Acts 28:2, NKJV). One translator says, 'Their kindness stood out like a star on a dark night'.

It was an act of kindness that helped bring me to Christ. I was a rebellious and defiant young man and always mischievous in Sunday school. At the end of the year, book prizes were given to all who attended Sunday school and, because of my bad behaviour and in order to teach me a lesson, the Sunday school committee decided that I would not be given a prize. It was a bad decision on their part because there would have been better and more Christian ways to deal with my bad behaviour than that, but let's leave that aside.

I was told of this well before the event and on prize-giving day I sat with the other boys and girls, not expecting anything. So you can imagine my surprise when my name was read out and I was called forward to receive my prize. I learned afterwards that my pastor, who also happened to be my uncle, had bought me a book out of his own money and slipped it into the box with all the other prize books. On the flyleaf he had written, 'Some people think you don't deserve a book but, despite your bad behaviour, I love you and want you to be included along with all the rest'. That action was filed in my memory and, years later, was used by the Holy Spirit to soften my heart and bring me to Christ.

Of course, it is also true that an *unkind* action can live on in the memory for a lifetime, but with different results. You know, in counselling we sometimes ask people what their biggest hurt was. We do that to identify some things that can help us in the counselling process. When I asked one woman, she told me that when she was a little girl she decided on her way home to pick some flowers in a field. Her mother was talking to a neighbour when she got home and when she gave her the flowers she, without a word of thanks, walked over to the rubbish bin, threw them in and went on talking. Yes, an act of unkindness can reverberate in someone for the whole of their life.

THIRDLY, KINDNESS SOMETIMES ACCOMPLISHES MORE THAN AN AUTHORITATIVE DEMAND

If you have the authority, you can make people do things they don't want to do by telling them to do it but, though they may obey, it is not done in a spirit of willingness. Like the little schoolboy, Johnny, who was feeling particularly rebellious one morning and remained standing in class after the teacher had told him to sit down.

'Johnny, sit down!' the teacher said a second time. Johnny was pretty defiant that morning so he remained standing. The third time the teacher raised his voice and said, 'This is the last time I am telling you. Sit down.' So Johnny sat down, but those sitting near him heard him mutter, 'I'm still standing up on the inside.'

Although God commands us to be kind, He goes further than that: He *exemplifies* it in the Person of His Son. A favourite verse of mine is found in Romans 2:4: '... *God's kindness is intended to lead you to repent* ...' (Amp). Imagine if God had never come to the world in the Person of His Son, Jesus Christ, but had simply shouted down to us from heaven through a megaphone, 'Repent!' How moved would we be by that approach, I wonder? But, no, He came into the world, wore our flesh, measured its frailty and earned the right to call us to repentance by His involvement in the messy business of living. He knows our condition because He has been *in* our condition.

How does the kindness of God lead us to repentance? Somebody has said that, if you wanted to represent Christianity in one English word and you were not able to use the word 'love', then the word 'kindness' would be the next best word. How kind God has been to us in giving His Son to die for us on the cross! If we can't use the word 'love' then surely we have to agree it is the kindest thing God could ever do for us.

Heaven's highest strategy for begetting a response in our hearts is to bring us to the cross and hold us there and, seeing God's kindness to us, our own hearts flame in response. I have found, as an evangelist, that the most powerful motivator in bringing people to Christ is to show them what God has done for them. That's why the greatest evangelistic text in the Bible is John 3:16: 'For God so loved the world that he gave his one and only Son, that whoever believes in him should not perish but have eternal life.'

Seeing how much we are loved we cry:

Amazing love how can it be
That thou my God should'st die for me?

Of course, we have to recognise that some people have confused ideas about kindness. They think they are being kind when really they are not; like the wife of the rich industrialist who, after listening to her husband's complaint concerning their chauffeur who had nearly killed him in his car, said 'Oh, don't dismiss him, dear! Give him one more chance.'

Let's look now at another phrase in the text: 'be *tenderhearted*'.

Some people have a tender heart by disposition. They are touched deeply by the world's needs and other people's problems. Others come to tenderheartedness through the gentle influences of the Holy Spirit working in them. In fact, I would go so far as to say that a Christian who is not tenderhearted is not a growing Christian. Some Christians excuse their lack of tenderness by saying, 'Well, I was born that way.' But we have been born again, haven't we? That should count for something, should it not?

Christianity promises a heart transplant: '*I will give you a new heart and put a new spirit within you* ...' (Ezek. 36:26). How does God do it? Well, He does it in answer to prayer. 'Soften my heart, Lord,' we sing, but we don't expect it actually to happen. Someone said that few Christians would ever think of telling lies in church, but they will sing them. How often do people pray that God will give them a heart that is tender? All too infrequently, in my experience. They will pray for more money, a better job and material things, but few come before God desperate to have a heart that is soft and tender. How sad. How very sad!

And now let's consider: '*forgiving one another*'.

This is where kindness is shown at its brightest and its best – in forgiveness. The word 'forgiveness' implies that there has been wrongdoing and Christians, like the rest of humanity, say and do wrong things to one another. Then comes the challenge to forgive and this is one of the greatest challenges of Christian living.

I had a tremendous test of this kind many years ago. A man who worked with me said some bad things about me and I resolved to make him sorry for what he had said. So I set out to make him squirm, and I was in a position to do this. I was able to put pressure on him and tighten the screws. But I found I couldn't pray with a disposition like this. I would try to pray but my words seemed to bounce back from the ceiling.

We just cannot get through to God when we hold unforgiveness in our hearts. 'If I regard iniquity in my heart,' said King David, 'the Lord will not hear' (Psa. 66:18, NKJV). God wouldn't even listen to me, let alone answer me. I gave up my vengeful attitude and behaviour and the power flowed through my life again almost instantly. Those of you who work with computers know what it is like when your modem is not working and you try to send an email. There is no connection. Then suddenly a connection is made and it begins to function again. I tell you, it's a wonderful moment when the power flows back into your life again because you resolve to forgive someone who has hurt you!

A woman I was counselling once said to me, 'I will never forgive that woman for what she did to me – *the cat*.' I said to her, 'I'm afraid you will have to or else you will never be able to pray again. Your Christian life will stop dead at this point and you won't go any further. Sing all the hymns and choruses you like but it won't work. Your soul will be soured and spoilt.' I'm glad to say she saw the point and made the decision to forgive.

Lastly, let's think about 'as *God in Christ has forgiven you*'.

Often my mind focuses on how much God has forgiven me for everything. Not almost everything or nearly everything, but EVERYTHING. Totally. Fully. Entirely. It is complete and absolute forgiveness.

The psalmist says in Psalm 103:12, 'as far as the east is from the west, so far has he removed our transgressions from us.' How total is that? Notice, it doesn't say 'as far as the north is from the south.' And there is good reason for that because, whilst there is a North Pole and a South Pole, there is no East Pole or West Pole.

Let me illustrate what is in my mind here. People who know me well are aware of my fascination with globes. Globes intrigue me much more than maps. Whilst looking at a globe one day, I ran my fingers down from the North Pole to the South Pole and then up again on the other side to the North Pole. I thought to myself, 'When I run my fingers down from the north, past the equator, how far do I have to go before I am going north again?' Well, as I kept going it was obvious: once I hit the South Pole I started going north again. Then I said to myself, 'How far do I have to go before I go south again?' Well, when I hit the North Pole the next direction was south.

Then I ran my finger from east to west along the equator and said, 'How far west do I have to go before I am going east?' The fact is, if I travel west and keep on going there is never a moment when I find myself going east. And vice versa. If I travel east there is never a moment when I find myself travelling west. The two never meet.

God's forgiveness is such that there is no danger of us ever meeting up with the sins of which we have been forgiven. And that is the kind of forgiveness we are to give to those who have hurt or wronged us.

So, hear the words again: 'even as *God in Christ forgave you*'. We are not to put people on probation and say, 'Come up to my expectations, or behave well in the future, and I will forgive you'. God doesn't deal with us like that and we are not to deal with others in that way either.

When people say, 'My problem is I can't forgive', I say, 'No, that's not your problem. Your problem is you don't know how much you have been forgiven. That's your problem'. When we see how much God has forgiven us, *really* see it, I mean, then the wonder of it is so powerful and motivating that we simply cannot hold back from forgiving others.

So, let's ensure that right now, in accordance with God's Word, all resentment and bitterness are emptied out of our hearts.

I came across this the other day in relation to resentment and found it quite striking: *Resentment is like drinking poison and expecting the other person to die.*

Let these most marvellous words from Scripture take hold of your soul today. Say them to yourself over and over again. Meditate on them until they become part of your thinking.

And be kind to one another, tenderhearted, forgiving one another, even as God in Christ forgave you.

3
THE SCARS OF
AN OLD WOUND

LUKE 1:5−25

In the time of Herod king of Judea there was a priest named
Zechariah, who belonged to the priestly division of Abijah;
his wife Elizabeth was also a descendant of Aaron. Both of
them were upright in the sight of God, observing all the Lord's
commandments and regulations blamelessly. But they had no
children, because Elizabeth was barren; and they were both
well on in years.

 Once when Zechariah's division was on duty and he was
serving as priest before God, he was chosen by lot, according
to the custom of the priesthood, to go into the temple of the
Lord and burn incense. And when the time for the burning
of incense came, all the assembled worshippers were praying
outside.

 Then an angel of the Lord appeared to him, standing at the
right side of the altar of incense. When Zechariah saw him,
he was startled and was gripped with fear. But the angel said
to him: 'Do not be afraid, Zechariah; your prayer has been
heard. Your wife Elizabeth will bear you a son, and you are
to give him the name John. He will be a joy and delight to
you, and many will rejoice because of his birth, for he will
be great in the sight of the Lord. He is never to take wine or
other fermented drink, and he will be filled with the Holy
Spirit even from birth. Many of the people of Israel will he
bring back to the Lord their God. And he will go on before
the Lord, in the spirit and power of Elijah, to turn the hearts
of the fathers to their children and the disobedient to the

wisdom of the righteous – to make ready a people prepared for the Lord.'

Zechariah asked the angel, 'How can I be sure of this? I am an old man and my wife is well on in years.'

The angel answered, 'I am Gabriel. I stand in the presence of God, and I have been sent to speak to you and to tell you this good news. And now you will be silent and not able to speak until the day this happens, because you did not believe my words, which will come true at their proper time.'

Meanwhile, the people were waiting for Zechariah and wondering why he stayed so long in the temple. When he came out, he could not speak to them. They realised he had seen a vision in the temple, for he kept making signs to them but remained unable to speak.

When his time of service was completed, he returned home. After this his wife Elizabeth became pregnant and for five months remained in seclusion. 'The Lord has done this for me,' she said. 'In these days he has shown his favour and taken away my disgrace among the people.'

This was probably the greatest day of Zechariah's life. He had what might be called a watershed day. Have you ever had a watershed day? You get up in the morning, go about your duties in the usual way and something happens that changes your whole life. For some of you, today might be a day like that.

Zechariah was a descendant of Aaron and, by virtue of that, was entitled to minister in the Temple as a priest. But there were so many priests in Jerusalem at this time that they were divided into twenty-four groups and, according to the first-century historian, Josephus, each group was given two weeks in a year to minister in the Temple. Each day the one to minister in the Holy Place was chosen by lot. This meant that, because of the lottery system, you could be a priest for a lifetime and never be chosen to go into the Holy Place! So it was always a dramatic moment when, at the beginning of the day, the ritual was performed to see on whom the lot would fall.

Imagine Zechariah's feelings as on this particular day the lot falls on him and he prepares to move into the Holy Place and minister to the Lord there. Consider for a moment something of the background to his situation.

Spiritually: it was a time of religious emptiness for Israel when no voice of a prophet was heard in the land. In fact, it had been 400 years since the last prophet had spoken. For 400 years Israel had been in a dark tunnel, so to speak, and no great light from heaven had pierced that darkness.

Politically: the throne was occupied by King Herod, an obnoxious and cruel despot whose merciless acts show him to have ruled in one of the blackest times of history.

Personally: Zechariah had for years carried a great problem in his heart. He had no sons or daughters because his wife was barren. I think we might safely assume that, being a servant of God, he had prayed many times that he and his wife Elizabeth would be given a child, but his prayers had not been answered. Now she was well past the age of childbearing and, therefore, humanly speaking, beyond hope.

He was working for God with a problem in his heart: I wonder if perhaps you are someone like that. You are engaged in ministry for the Lord but inwardly you are struggling with an issue that tends to drain your physical energy, vitiate your spiritual resources and paralyse your best and noblest intentions.

It needs to be said, I think, that not every problem we encounter in our lives needs to be resolved. I have come to the conclusion, after a lifetime of trying to help people with their problems, that there are two kinds of problem that arise in the lives of believers: those that God puts in our way to deepen and develop our characters and those that arise from the circumstances of life that He wants to help us overcome.

I have often told my students that the primary goal of biblical counselling is not the solution of problems. It is a common, but I think erroneous, belief in the field of people-helping that one starts with the presenting problem and works one's way towards a resolution. But that's the wrong place to start. A more basic issue is to back up and ask: What is God seeking to do in this person's life and how can I co-operate with Him?

I ask my student counsellors: Do you understand that your primary task is not to resolve problems but to deal with them in harmony with what God wants? I have found myself saying to people time and time again: I think you are going to have to live with this problem for some time, perhaps even a lifetime, as I think God is using it to deepen your character and advance His purposes in your life. My task is to support you in this and pray with you that you may absorb the grace that God promises to give you.

Imagine yourself, for a moment, as a biblical counsellor living in the days of Paul, and he comes to you for help with the problem he speaks of in 2 Corinthians 12: a thorn in the flesh. If your primary goal is to resolve his problem you will be working against the purposes of God, for God will not remove it despite your best efforts. People today will want help to resolve their problems whilst effective biblical counsellors will want to explore why they are there. So, biblical counsellors must accept unpopularity. The fact is that most people are more interested in finding relief than finding God in the midst of the problem.

Some time ago I talked to someone well known in the counselling world. He had been trying to see me for months but, because I was undergoing pretty heavy cancer therapy at the time, I was unable to see him. He pressed me hard to talk to him, even being prepared to delay an overseas trip. So, we talked, and I came to sense that the very thing he wanted to have removed was, in fact, acting like a thorn in the flesh in his life. It was helping to keep him humble. I said, 'I don't think God wants to remove this from your life. It is your thorn in the flesh to keep you humble. Without that you would not have the great ministry you have.' So, some problems need resolving, others don't.

What was the issue with which Zechariah needed help? I think it was a much bigger issue than that his wife was barren. It goes more deeply than that to the issue of his concept of God, his confidence in the Almighty and, probably, a lingering disappointment in his heart.

As Zechariah moves into the Holy Place an angel appears to him. All this is going on and suddenly an angel appears! What would you do right now if an angel appeared in the room? Personally, I have never seen an angel. Some of my friends claim to have seen one but, for me, that pleasure has never been realised. The angel tells him, 'You and Elizabeth are going to have a child.' He is stunned by this news. Now there is a clash of mixed emotions inside him: astonishment, fear, trepidation, alarm, perhaps surprise.

Here was an angel telling him that he was about to receive a miracle. Later we read of an angel appearing to Mary, the mother of Jesus, who responded in a quite different way. Zechariah had mixed emotions such as we all experience from time to time.

Let me freeze the frame right there.

Here was an angel telling Zechariah that the thing he had desired and prayed for was now going to happen. But he appears unable to believe it or receive it. Even though he is a priest and ministering in the Temple, his faith doesn't seem to be able to rise to the occasion. This is what he had prayed for and longed for, but now he didn't seem able to reach out and receive it.

His response is: 'How can I be sure of this? I am an old man and my wife is well on in years' (v.18). Why, in the presence of an angel, does Zechariah find it so difficult to believe that what the celestial being says is going to happen *will* happen? As a priest, he knew the history of the God of Israel who had opened up seas, sent fire down from heaven, raised the dead and so on. Surely it was just a little thing for God to touch the womb of his wife, Elizabeth. I can only speculate, but I wonder if he was experiencing what so many people experience when something they long for has not happened and, because of the disappointment they experience, they fear they might be disappointed again.

Often, in the counselling room, I have observed the strange spectacle of someone who longs for something and then, when God offers it, they are unable to receive it – the incredible action of someone holding back at the very place they want to move forward!

Why would that be? I have come to believe that the causes of many of our problems in life are not intellectual but emotional. Feelings rise up that frighten us and, in order to deal with those feelings, we intellectualise them, so that we can more easily wrestle with them. Like the young man who said to me, 'I am finding great difficulty in accepting certain parts of Scripture.' His problem was not really intellectual for, underlying that statement, were emotions of deep guilt arising out of his unbiblical lifestyle. Emotions can sometimes overwhelm our reasoning.

I once said to a young man on a plane who had told me he didn't believe in God, 'Tell me the kind of God you don't believe in and maybe I'll find that I don't believe in him either.'

He said, 'I don't believe in a God who sends tidal waves to drown people and organises famines and all kinds of terrible things.'

To which I then said, 'It might surprise you that I don't believe in a God who does this either.'

It took a bit of explaining and covering of some theological points but I think he came to see that the way he felt about God caused him to disbelieve in God. I say again: emotions can sometimes overwhelm our reasoning.

What emotions were reverberating in Zechariah, I wonder, that were overwhelming his view of God? Was it hurt, indignation, resentment or disappointment rising up within him to prevent him from reaching out and accepting what was now being offered?

Through experience I have come to see that emotions play a big part in our lives. But there is a strange teaching in some quarters of the Christian Church that, whenever an unacceptable emotion arises, you are to pretend it is not there, to deny it. This is spiritually and psychologically unhealthy. There is too much pretence amongst the people of God. You don't have to indulge in negative emotions but you do have to admit to them. Integrity requires that whatever is true must be faced. Some Christians read texts like 'be not angry' and therefore, even though they are angry, they pretend they are not. But you can never change what you don't acknowledge.

Remember Jeremiah? When he was angry with God, did the Lord tumble off His throne? No, He allowed Jeremiah to get mad at Him. Jeremiah effectively said, 'God you tricked me – when I was a little boy you said this ... and now here you are ...' Then, as he thought about it, the word that God had given him began to burn in his heart. (See Jeremiah 20.)

I remember a man telling me once, when I was pastor of a church, that he had fallen in love with another woman in the church. His own marriage was loveless and he said, 'Please help me, pastor. I find myself thinking about this woman, imagining we are together. I do not fantasise about having sex with her but thoughts of her fill my mind continually.' I took him through some in-depth counselling which involved memorising certain parts of Scripture and countering the unacceptable thoughts with the Word of God. Weeks later I asked him how things were going and he said, 'I still find thoughts rising within me, and sometimes they scream out with fierce intensity, but when they do I find that ... that God's Word screams the loudest!' Wow!

A book I found good to read is *The Emotional Quotient* by Daniel Goleman – a bestseller in the USA some years ago. He points out that people often fail in life, not because of lack of intellect, but because they cannot handle their emotions. I often think of Ahithophel, who was a friend of David and also the grandfather of Bathsheba whom David seduced. He was so affected by the emotions of this event, I believe, that, even though he was a friend, there came a time when the tide turned and he offered to chase after David and kill him. When that didn't work out, knowing that David was aware of his plot, he committed suicide. I wonder if the lingering resentment caused him to do that.

Now I ask the question again: what was Zechariah's problem? As a counsellor, I have often wondered if what I am now going to suggest might have been going on inside him. He wanted a child and his wife's barrenness was something of a stigma in those days. But now he is being told all this is going to change and he just can't believe it, even though it is an angel who is telling him this. What had dulled his sensitivities and demoralised him in his faith?

Let me bring in at this point something written by Os Guinness. He said, 'Imagine you have cut yourself in the palm of your hand. Soon a scar is there and it is sensitive for a while. You grab a knife and it isn't quite healed yet and as it touches the unhealed wound in your hand you wince with the small amount of pain and drop the knife. You drop it because there is something going on that has not yet healed.'

Our souls have the same problem. Perhaps some disappointment of the past: God never came through in the way you thought He should and you hesitate to give yourself fully to Him. Oh, you go on working for Him, but there is doubt and difficulty in your heart. Maybe, having been disappointed once, you can't stretch out with the hand of faith even though God is talking to you – as He is at this moment. All because of some hurt of the past which you have never dealt with. It is there, in the palm of your spiritual hand, discouraging you from reaching out again in case it might not be true and you might be hurt again.

We get a vivid example of this in Luke 24. Here's a text I bet you have never heard a sermon on! Picture the scene with me: the disciples are huddled together in the Upper Room like frightened sheep in a pen when, suddenly, the risen and radiant Jesus appears before them. They are startled and afraid. He shows them His hands and feet and says, 'Touch me.' They are overcome with emotions, but they are mixed emotions. The Scriptures say in verse 41: '... while they still did not believe it because of joy ...' What does that mean? It's a startling scripture. Listen to it again: '... while they still did not believe it because of joy ...'

They wanted to believe it was the Lord, but they were afraid to give themselves fully to the idea just in case it might not be so. The prospect of being disappointed again was so fearful that they hardly dared to believe.

And so the disciples are caught in this strange situation where they prefer the safety of doubt to the risk of disappointment. They were still adjusting to the shock of the news that Jesus had risen from the dead, and the prospect of the pain they would feel if it were not true was so overwhelming that, for a moment, they could not give themselves to the idea that it really was the Lord. One translation says: 'It seemed too good to be true.' Before the sedative of time had dulled their pain they were being opened up to a new challenge.

At any given moment certain emotions exist within me. If there are emotions that are painful for me to admit to, I am capable of disowning them, pretending they are not there or refusing to deal with them consciously. I say again, you don't have to *indulge* unacceptable emotions, but you do have to admit to them.

In my experience, Christians constantly go in and out of denial. This has surprised me more than anything in my Christian life. Perhaps 60 per cent of Christians live in denial. Not entirely, of course, but far too much for them to be healthy Christians. I believe denial is an attempt to dethrone God. We are not sure God can handle the real world so we change it by denying it or spiritualising it.

I think of how often people have said to me, 'I am confused.' Then, later, they come up with the most nonsensical explanation because even nonsensical answers are better than no answer. Confusion erodes our sense of competence and being in control. Trust is not easy. Denial distorts life in order to make us feel more comfortable.

I want to deal with problems in ways that honour God and are faithful to Scripture. Here are the three suggestions I give to people in relation to painful emotions:

- Face them and feel them
- Discover how they arose
- Choose to express them in accordance with biblical guidelines

I have seen many Christians in the position where some emotion associated with hurt or confusion or misunderstanding in the past rises up to hinder them from reaching out for what is being offered. Thus they hold back, even though they long, above everything, to move forward.

It's interesting how we cushion ourselves against disappointment and by that very cushioning we deprive ourselves of moving on with God.

It is reported that Victor Banerjee, star of the film *A Passage to India*, said when he got the script that he didn't want to read it because of the disappointment he would feel if he did not get the part. You see college or university students doing this as they say: 'I don't think I will get very good marks because of ... this or that or the other.' They are cushioning themselves against disappointment in this way.

A healthy faith is a faith that holds on to God with a firm grip like Mary, the mother of Jesus, who reached out and took hold of God with a healthy grip. What purity and love and faith this young woman had for God.

Now, can I ask you what great pain you might be risking if you were to reach out and touch God in a new way? Is there some disappointment in your life because God didn't come through for you in the way you thought He should? Has He been too long in answering the prayer of your heart? Are you upset with Him for allowing people to hurt you and do you go about your tasks dutifully but without any joy or passion in your heart? Perhaps some official in the church, some deacon, some colleague, has hurt you and you can't trust another human being?

Someone may have let you down and you can't be vulnerable anymore. Maybe you have been let down in love and will not allow yourself to love again. You prefer the safety of doubt to the risk of disappointment.

I was brought up to believe that the root of sin is rebellion, but Oswald Chambers changed my mind when he said, 'The root of sin is the suspicion that God is not good.' He moved the primary issue from the will to the emotions. If I understand the personality aright, it is our thinking that affects the way we feel and our feelings that affect the choices we make. It can be put like this: what I think about affects the way I feel. The thought that perhaps God is not good is powerful. Oswald Chambers points out that in the Garden of Eden what produced the Fall was the fact that Adam and Eve did not believe God had their highest interests at heart, and that thought of not being considered by God produced emotions that brought about capitulation in the personality. Now you may reject that but, personally, I think it makes a lot of sense.

We live today in a world where the data showing that God is good is not all that convincing. We see His majesty in creation, but God lets little babies be abused and, when we think of His permissive will, we realise He could have intervened if He had wanted to. And then there are times when God doesn't answer prayers, which causes us to wonder whether He is really as good as He says He is.

Do you know what I do when I find these thoughts circulating in my being? I come back to the fact of the cross and dwell on the truth that a God who gave His Son to die for me has got to be good. I love the story that my mentor Dr W.E. Sangster used to tell of the boy who went with his friends to a youth camp where he soon ran out of money. He sent a telegram to his father: 'SOS LSD RSVP.' (Some of you may be too young to remember that LSD was the currency we used before decimalisation!) However, nothing came and his friends taunted him, 'Your father doesn't love you.' He replied, 'I know my father and when I get home he will tell me his reasons himself.' Then, sure enough, when he got home his father, with tears in his eyes, said, 'I knew you needed to understand the value of money and so I thought this would be a wonderful time to teach you.' The answer the boy gave to his school friends is the answer I give to people who ask why God allows certain things: I will wait until I get home to know the reason why and He will tell me Himself.

I have met so many Christians who have pushed down their feelings of disappointment with God over something that happened in the past. They never deal with it but stuff it into the unconscious. We never bury an emotion dead – it is always alive. This is why we must face our emotions, feel them and wrestle with them, if necessary, until we come to the realisation that God knows best. Change the 'd' in disappointment to 'h' and what do you get? His appointment!

Who amongst us has not met the difficult issue of thwarted plans, things not turning out the way one expected, and so on. It was Oswald Chambers who said also that life is more tragic than orderly.

God is all-powerful. But Christians know that, in the midst of the greatest catastrophe, we are called to believe that God has not lost His power and could intervene if He wished, but that He has allowed it to happen for an overall good and wise purpose. And it is tough believing that in the face of some situations which God allows.

Our concept of God is crucial to our growth. You will never rise higher than your concept of God. You tell me how you see God and I can almost predict the problems you will experience in your life.

Many times in my life I have got upset with God because He wasn't running my life the way I thought He ought to and I have said, 'Lord, you don't love me.' But He has always come to me and bidden me gaze at the cross. And there, as I see how much I am loved, the scales fall from my eyes and my own love flames in response. Oh yes! A God who gave His life for me on the cross has got to be good.

How does God deal with us when He wants to advance His purposes in our lives and He knows that we are going to have difficulty in accepting His instructions because of the scars of an old wound in our hands?

FIRSTLY, HE WILL FIND A WAY OF GETTING TO US THROUGH ONE OF HIS REPRESENTATIVES

God will find a way to speak to us and get to us, even if He has to turn the world upside down – metaphorically speaking, of course! In Zechariah's case He sent an angel.

God's commitment to us is quite wonderful. He has invested so much in us that He will not let go of us. We give up so easily on Him but He will not give up on us. In some of the times of confusion in my life, when I have been wondering which way to go and couldn't hear from God because my anxieties blocked the communication channels, God has sent someone to me to give me a word of direction. He has never failed.

Many years ago (in the 1960s), as I was considering establishing a church in central London, an evangelist friend of mine from the USA was getting on a plane in Tokyo and God said to him, 'Go to London and give this message to Selwyn Hughes.' He changed his flight, came to London and said, 'God says you are to go ahead with the desires in your heart and He will make a way for you.' Wow!

Now I have a message for you. I am not an angel (you have probably guessed that anyway), however, I was once mistaken for an angel. In Yorkshire, where pastors didn't wait for someone to come to the door but just knocked and walked in, I called at a house and when I walked in I heard from upstairs the voice of the lady of the house, who, thinking her husband had just come home, shouted, 'Is that you, angel?' 'No,' I responded, 'but I'm from the same department!'

God will find a way to speak to you if He has something He wants you to do. He is committed to you and will not give up on you. I stand like that angel who spoke to Zechariah in the presence of God and speak to you in His name: 'Is there disappointment in your life – some disappointment over your call, perhaps – and now God is talking to you? Is there some resentment against God because He allowed something to happen that you thought He should have shielded you from?' Sometimes it is only the call that we have to hold on to. He will not leave us to experience confusion for too long.

SECONDLY, HE WILL SPEAK LOVINGLY BUT STRONGLY TO US

Although God is kind and compassionate, this will not stop Him from confronting us in the strongest and most direct manner whenever that is appropriate. There are many issues in Scripture, I have found, where God, or Christ, confronts His servants in a strong manner. Take as an example the case of the church in Laodicea. The church was lukewarm. And how does Christ address them? He says, 'You make me sick!' That's how one translation puts it. You might be more familiar with the phrase: 'I will spew you out of my mouth!' Why does He talk in such confrontational language? Because lukewarm people need to be shocked. Being lukewarm is a perilous spiritual condition. Lukewarm people say, 'I am not cold. I have an element of warmth. I am not lifeless. I don't go to extremes. I am in control.' But you are not hot either – and Jesus said of such people, 'You make me sick!'

Often God's voice is hindered from getting deep into our souls because of self-pity. I think this is where Zechariah was, and self-pity, believe me, is another perilous spiritual condition. You see, self-pity says, 'Poor me! Life really seems to be down on me.' It is easily the most destructive of the non-pharmaceutical narcotics. It soothes the pain, gives momentary relief and separates the victim from reality, but it does not heal. It's surprising how much better we feel when we pity ourselves. But self-pity and self-contempt (a similar dynamic) is a humanistic way of dealing with pain in the soul and a substitute for bringing it to God and letting Him deal with it in His own way.

Zechariah's self-pity and his whining about being an old man do not impress the angel of God. 'All right,' says the angel, speaking firmly, yet compassionately, 'God's purposes are going to come to pass but, because you are having trouble believing the words of God and you can't speak words of faith, then until the miracle comes to pass you will be dumb! If you can't respond with words of faith then you won't be able to speak any words at all.'

My! I'm glad God doesn't act like that these days or many of God's servants, like us, would get up in the pulpit on a Sunday and when we open our mouths nothing would come out.

THIRDLY, GOD DEMONSTRATES HIS FAITHFULNESS AND WILL NOT GIVE UP ON HIS PURPOSES FOR US EVEN THOUGH SOMETIMES WE MIGHT GIVE UP ON HIM

I'm so glad that, though God confronts us, He doesn't give up on us. This is what C.S. Lewis called 'the intolerable compliment'. God loves us as we are but He loves us too much to let us stay as we are. He faces us with the reality of the situation and, even though He has to challenge us, His love for us comes shining through. 'It's going to happen, Zechariah, and though you cannot accept it now you will see it come to pass and then you will speak words of praise and power.'

I'm so glad, too, that God always brings this message home to our hearts: 'I'm not angry with you. I love you. It's your highest interests I have at heart even though you stumble over My words and My actions.' In one way or another He will keep reminding us of that, time and time again.

We are wounded healers. But it is the *cleansing* of our wounds that is important. Christ's wounds are healed. He was scorned (and even had a group of disciples who must have disappointed Him at times) but He would allow no resentment to remain in Him and with his dying breath He said, 'Father, forgive them.'

Sometimes, because of the disappointments of the past, we hover in a state of uncertainty, afraid to move towards the divine beckoning or approach to us in case we might be disappointed again. It's a form of 'spiritual agoraphobia', a fear of the wide-open spaces, which makes us stay safely shut in.

What is happening in your life that can only be accounted for by God? When anyone asks me that question I reply, '*Every Day with Jesus*'. How can I have been writing this single-handedly for forty years without missing an issue? God is the only answer.

I know what it means to be disappointed and hurt. I know what it is to wonder whether God called me to the ministry and I came close, at one time, to leaving it. I know what it is to have to wait years for God to bring to pass something He promised me, and which I thought He had forgotten. I know the bitterness that rose up in my heart, which I would not admit to, but was there nevertheless. I know what it is to stand at the side of the coffin of the woman I married and say 'goodbye' and to bury my only two sons within ten months of each other, and wonder why all these things happened.

But I also know what it means to reach out with the unhealed scars of an old wound in my hand, offer them to Him for healing and take a firm grip on the hand of God.

If you are in the condition I describe (and many of you are), then offer your self-pity to Him, and your bitterness, resentment, indignation, disappointment, and let Him heal them. Reach up to Him. And as you reach up with the scars of an old wound in your hand, look ... look ... there are hands that reach down to take hold of yours. And watch carefully. There are scars in His hands too. But they are *healed* scars. There is no resentment against those who crucified Him. No disappointment that things didn't go His way. He trusted God in everything and that is why, if you offer Him your hurts and disappointments –

HIS SCARS WILL HEAL YOUR SCARS.

~4~
WISHING, WANTING, WILLING

LUKE 11:1–13

And it came to pass, as He was praying in a certain place, when He ceased, that one of His disciples said to Him, 'Lord, teach us to pray, as John also taught his disciples.' So He said to them, 'When you pray, say:

Our Father in heaven,

Hallowed be Your name.

Your kingdom come.

Your will be done,

On earth as it is in heaven.

Give us day by day our daily bread.

And forgive us our sins,

For we also forgive everyone who is indebted to us.

And do not lead us into temptation,

But deliver us from the evil one.'

And He said to them, 'Which of you shall have a friend, and go to him at midnight and say to him, "Friend, lend me three loaves; for a friend of mine has come to me on his journey, and I have nothing to set before him"; and he will answer from within and say, "Do not trouble me; the door is now shut, and my children are with me in bed; I cannot rise and give to you"? I say to you, though he will not rise and give to him because he is his friend, yet because of his persistence he will rise and give him as many as he needs.

'And I say to you, ask, and it will be given to you; seek, and you will find; knock, and it will be opened to you. For everyone who asks receives, and he who seeks finds, and to him who knocks it will be opened. If a son asks for bread from any father among you, will he give him a stone? Or if he asks for a fish, will he give him a serpent instead of a fish? Or if he asks for an egg, will he offer him a scorpion? If you then, being evil, know how to give good gifts to your children, how much more will your heavenly Father give the Holy Spirit to those who ask Him!' (NKJV)

One of the things that used to puzzle me greatly when I was a young Christian was the fact that so many of my fellow believers that I met never seemed to get what they wanted spiritually. I was always a questioning teenager and I used to say to people, 'How's your prayer life going? What kind of answers do you get?' And many times people would say to me something like this: 'Well I've asked the Lord for this but I've still not received it.' And the things that we would be talking about would not be those things about which there might be some doubt that God would want to give them, but things like faith, love, the Holy Spirit and so on.

So for a while, as a young Christian, I struggled to balance the apparent contradiction between a large-hearted God and the seeming impoverishment of so many Christians. I came across this so much in the early days of my Christian life that I leaned towards a kind of hyper-Calvinism that led me to believe that maybe God did have favourites and that some were predestined to receive and others were not. And then I pulled away from that and veered to the opposite view, that some people were naturally good receivers. So I oscillated and vacillated between these two views for a number of years and then I discovered a spiritual principle that resolved the issue for me once and for all. It was this: that true spiritual fulfilment comes in proportion to the degree of our spiritual desire. It was Jeremiah who put this into focus for me. We read, 'You will seek me and find me when you seek me with all your heart' (Jer. 29:13). And Jesus built that same principle into the Sermon on the Mount when He said, 'Blessed are those who hunger and thirst for righteousness for they will be filled' (Matt. 5:6). Now I don't know if our Lord had in mind people not receiving what they should receive, spiritually, but His words certainly address the question of why some Christians don't receive all they should be receiving from God and others do.

Jesus, in the passage we are considering from Luke's Gospel, gives us not merely a form of prayer but a whole philosophy about prayer. And if we are not receiving from God the things that we know He wants to give us, and if there is some block or obstacle in our lives, then we have to ask ourselves two questions. The first is this: is the fault in God? To which the answer must be NO. Jesus, you see, clears the mists and the misconceptions that may surround the nature of God by the use of two very powerful metaphors: He calls Him 'Our Father' and He also refers to Him as a friend.

Now I have come to believe that our concept of God is one of the most determinative aspects of our spiritual lives. Before we get down on our knees to pray we ought to ask ourselves what kind of God we are praying to. For the way you see God affects the way you will ask Him and believe for the things that He wants to give. You will never rise higher in your Christian life, I believe, than your concept of God. You tell me your concept of God and I can almost predict the problems that you are going to experience in your prayer life and also in your relationships with other people. For we are made and moulded by the image of God that we carry in our hearts, and I discovered this in the counselling room. I discovered that so many emotional problems can be traced back to a faulty concept of God.

'How do you see God?' I asked a girl on one occasion, and she said, 'I see Him sitting behind a newspaper.' Now do you need three guesses to know where her father spent his time? The fact is that very often the image of God we carry in our hearts has developed from our early relationships. I remember, on another occasion, asking a woman, 'What is the image that the word "God" brings to you – not the intellectual idea, but the feelings you have?' And she said, 'Cold, distant and uncommunicative.' Half an hour later I said, 'Tell me what your father was like,' and she used the same three words to describe him – cold, distant and uncommunicative. One of the things that has amazed me in my life as a pastor and a counsellor is that so often I have been able to trace emotional ill-health back to a faulty concept of God.

You may not understand how it is that a faulty concept of God can sabotage your spiritual life, but listen to the following words. They are by Dr Joseph Cook, a brilliant anthropologist with a PhD from the University of Seattle in Washington, who gave it all up to go to Thailand as a missionary. While he was there he had a breakdown and was invalided back to the US. After a long period of counselling he wrote about his recovery in a book called *Free for the Taking* (now out of print, unfortunately). This is what he wrote:

I invented an impossible God whose demands of me were so mighty, and His opinion of me so low, that there was no way to live except under His frown. All day long He nagged me – why don't you pray more? Why don't you witness more? When will you ever learn self-discipline? How can you allow yourself to indulge in such wicked thoughts? Do this. Do that. Don't do this. Don't do that. Yield. Confess. Work harder. God was always using His love against me. He'd show me His nail-pierced hands – look at me glaringly and say – why aren't you a better Christian? Get busy and live the way that you ought to. I had a God who down underneath considered me less than dirt. He would make a great show about loving me but I believed that the day-to-day love and acceptance I longed for could only be mine if I let Him crush everything that was really me. When it came down to it there was scarcely a word or a thought or a feeling or a decision of mine that God really liked.

Now do you wonder why a man like that would have a breakdown? Well, I don't, because I have seen it happen so many times. You see, he saw God as a slave driver and that was the way he served Him. He was serving not the true God but a caricature. He was out on the mission field to help people turn from idols to serve the true and living God, but he himself was bowing down to an idea and a concept of God that was spun out of his childhood fears and guilts and inner confusion. He would have said that he would never dream of bowing down to an idol of wood or of stone but, without realising it, he was bowing down to an image of God that was constructed out of the raw materials of his guilts and fears. You see, by some secret law of the soul, we become like the God we serve. And you can't really give yourself to a God whom you do not respect.

Martin Luther said to some theologians who were talking about God, 'What you describe as God I would describe as the devil.' He added, 'You are describing God like a slave driver, driving His sheep to the abattoir, not as a shepherd who leads His sheep into the green pastures.'

Some years ago, on my only visit to Japan, en route to Korea, I was speaking to a group of missionaries before going on to the airport. One of them asked if she could come to the airport with me so that she could talk with me. I had a taxi waiting, and she offered to pay the fare to the airport – which seemed like a good deal to me – so I agreed. As we sat together she told me: 'I do not believe that God will listen to me and I feel that He is not pleased with me unless I am working myself to death, labouring under some sickness or at the point of exhaustion with my work'. I said to her, 'Let me describe to you what kind of parents you had', and I gave her a five-minute description, to which she responded, 'How did you know that?' My charismatic friends would call that a word of knowledge, my non-charismatic friends would call it divine insight! I don't care what you call it, but I know that there is a very simple explanation. You see, when we are converted, God doesn't come down and drill a hole in the top of our heads and insert a new tape that changes the way we think about Him! We tend to relate to God in the way that we related to authority figures, especially our parents, in our early developmental years. So often, when people come into the Christian life, they begin to see God and relate to Him just as they saw and related to these authority figures in their lives. It is amazing how this happens! A minister I once counselled had suffered ten breakdowns. He was brought up by parents who were impossible to please and then he exchanged his parents for his church and told himself, 'I have got to make a hundred visits a week or else God will not love me'.

Once I asked a woman, 'Supposing you lay down on the floor and didn't wake up for a whole year, but were kept alive by a life-support machine, do you think that God would love you as much when you woke up as when you went to sleep?' And she said, 'Of course not!' 'Why?' I asked. 'Well,' she said, 'I wouldn't have been to church or read my Bible and I wouldn't have been praying'. I said to her, 'Do you realise

God loves you for who you are and not just for what you do?' What we do *is* important, and I want to stress this, but God loves us not just for what we do but for *who we are in Jesus Christ*.

Now, can you see how important our concept of God is to our spiritual lives, to our growth and to our development as Christians? There is a verse in Hebrews that says, '... for he who comes to God must believe that He is, and that He is a rewarder of those who diligently seek Him' (11:6, NKJV). But what if I hold in my heart an image of God as cold and distant and uncommunicative? Then, when I get down on my knees to ask Him for something, the energy of my soul is short-circuited by the fact that I am not sure that He wants to give me what I ask for. If I am not sure that He delights to give, then my asking will be shot through with uncertainty and doubts and misgivings.

There's a story that we tell in Wales about a farmer called David Jones. One day his tractor gave up on him and across the fields, on another farm, was a friend of his by the name of Tom Jones. (There are lots of Tom Joneses in Wales!) So he thought, 'I will walk across the fields and see if I can borrow his tractor.' As he went along he was thinking to himself, 'Now, Tom is not a very generous kind of person, and there was an occasion many years ago in the village when someone was in trouble and everybody got together to help but Tom never did anything about it. He is the kind of person who is a little mean and a little niggardly and parsimonious.' As he walked he said to himself, 'Now, I wonder, will he really loan me his tractor? I guess he will come up with a dozen reasons why he can't give it to me today.' Eventually, his mind filled with these thoughts, he arrived at the farmhouse door and knocked on it and when Tom Jones came to the door he said, 'I've come to tell you that you can keep your jolly old tractor!'

Now it is so important, when we ask God for things, that we have a right concept of Him. Jesus makes it clear that when it comes to giving to His children, God is *not* mean. He is *not* niggardly. The Almighty, says Jesus, delights to give to His children. He is large-hearted, magnanimous, overflowing with eagerness to respond to the legitimate requests of His children. Listen to this: *'If you then, being evil, know how to give good gifts to your children, how much more will your heavenly Father give the Holy Spirit to those who ask Him!'* (NKJV). Now, tell me, is there anything a parent delights to do more than give to their child something they know their child longs for and that is good for them? Those of you who are parents recognise what Jesus is saying. So, take that feeling of delight you have when you can give to your child the thing he or she longs for, and that you know is good for them, multiply it a million times, and you get a faint picture of the joy and the pleasure that flows through the heart of God when He can respond to the needs of His children. *'... how much more will your heavenly Father ...'*: There is a kind of a divine transformer that takes the feeling in the heart of a parent and boosts it to a level of passion and intensity that is unimaginable. No, if you are not receiving in your spiritual life from God, the fault is not in Him. He is large-hearted, magnanimous! He delights to give! What Jesus is saying here is that the Father so delights to give that, if you are not receiving, then it is not His fault and therefore it must be yours. If you are not receiving spiritually in the way that you should, then mark this, and mark it well, it is not God's fault.

It is here that I must now bring you face to face with another word from Jeremiah: not only did God say, 'You will seek me and find me when you seek me with all your heart' (Jer. 29:13), but He also said this: 'The heart is deceitful above all things, and desperately wicked: who can know it? I, the LORD search the heart ...' (Jer. 17:9–10, AV).

You know, I always see my greatest task as a pastor and a counsellor as uncovering the subterfuges of the human heart – and there is no deception worse than self-deception. We can actually deceive ourselves (and we need to understand this) into believing that we want something from God when really we are not quite sure that we want it. Does that surprise you? We can deceive ourselves so easily in that.

I was a pastor in Yorkshire, in the North of England, and one day I went to the factory not too far away from my church, where there were hundreds of girls working. I went to the manager and I said, 'Look, I'd like to run a "singsong" for half an hour and teach these girls some Christian choruses.' I used to play the accordion at that time and I took this along with me and the manager of the factory allowed me to go into the canteen. They had an hour for lunch, during which I gathered them all together and said, 'Let me teach you some songs.' I taught them some bright and lively choruses and, after doing this for a few weeks, I said to them, 'Now, I would like you to come to my church on Sunday. I've been coming to you, so why don't you come to my church?' And, the following Sunday night, 150 young girls streamed into the church, all dressed up in their usual style, and scared the life out of the Christians who were there! That same night 100 of them gave their lives to Jesus Christ. I was pastor to them for several years and helped them to develop in their Christian life and, you know, if you have 100 girls, it is not long before you have 100 boys coming into the church! I had to say to them, 'Look, you really belong to another church and we don't have room here.' But young people kept coming in and soon the young men and women who had been converted began to pair up together and I conducted two or three weddings a week for almost two years in this particular place.

There was one young girl who didn't have a boyfriend and she came to me and asked me to pray that God would give her one. I suggested we get down upon our knees to pray together, and as I began to pray I suddenly had a thought. I said, 'Let's sit down.' Then, facing her, I said, very gently, 'You don't want a boyfriend, do you?' 'What do you mean?' she said, 'I have just asked you to pray for a boyfriend.' 'But that's not what you want,' I repeated. 'Explain yourself. What do you mean?' she said. I remembered what I had observed as she went around the church, that she had a way of saying things to young men that would cause them to walk away from her and reject her. She would talk to them in such a way that, very quickly, they would back away from her or turn away. I had noticed this and wondered to myself what was going on inside her that made her have this way of putting people off and causing them to reject her. Those of you who know anything about the workings of the personality will know that she was getting what she wanted deep down in her heart. She was actually setting herself up for rejection.

When I talked to her I found out that, growing up in her family, she had been rejected. She was one of five sisters and her father's nickname for her was 'The Devil's Daughter'. All her life she had been rejected, and rejection had become so much part of her relationships that it was the only thing she felt comfortable with. As this feeling of being rejected was the only feeling that she knew, in all her relationships she was actually setting herself up for it. And she was doing it unconsciously. She was preferring the safety of the familiar to the risk and the adventure of some new feelings. She was preventing those feelings that might come into her life if she were to allow herself to open up to experience and understand the serendipity of love – the surprises that come to us as we move towards people and experience in our relationships, especially those first-love relationships of our teenage years.

I said to her, 'Can you see what you are doing, that you are setting yourself up for rejection? This is the way you work: you say that you want a boyfriend with your lips but, deep down inside you, what you really want is to re-experience those feelings that have been going on all your life, with which you are so familiar.' She admitted she had never realised this and asked, 'How do I get out of this?' It actually took hours of counselling to get her to the place where she began to be willing to move towards people and take the risk of new relationships and learning new things.

One interpretation of the passage from Luke that we are considering is that, when you ask God for something and you don't receive it, you must heighten your enthusiasm and passion in seeking and, if you still don't get it, then you hammer at the gates of heaven and persist in doing so until you receive it. That's the traditional view, but it's not one with which I can agree.

Many years ago I came across the book, *Nature, Man and God*, by a great Archbishop of Canterbury of the last century, William Temple. This book is so intense that I can only take in a few sentences at a time, and I keep it by my bedside because it is a sure remedy for insomnia! Whenever I can't get to sleep I read a page of this and I can guarantee that within minutes I will be fast asleep. William Temple was one of our great evangelical archbishops and, sadly, not many of his successors have been as strong and evangelical in their faith as he was. What a shame it was that we lost him during the time of the Second World War. What I read in his book that transformed my thinking as a pastor is this: that we wish for things, we want things, but often our true willing is in another direction and it is here we must examine our hearts, for the prayers of our lips are often opposite to the prayers of our hearts. If we are not receiving from God the things that we know beyond doubt He desires to give us, then we must ruthlessly examine ourselves at each level. God can't make us more holy than we *will* to be. We receive as much as we will for and as little as we are satisfied with. So it is not just wishing in prayer, it is not just wanting, it is *willing*, and our true willing goes on deep down inside us. What we get is not simply what we ask for with our lips but what we *really* desire, deep down in our hearts.

Here is an illustration of this. A young man at Bristol University in England came to see me some years ago. He had, he told me, an IQ of 150, but he was failing in his examinations and had come to ask for my help. I had no idea what was going on. Here was a man with an IQ of 150 and yet he was failing in his examinations! I prayed, and the Lord showed me what was going on in his heart. So I invited him back and I asked him, 'Why are you so bitter against your parents?' Astonished, he said, 'How did you know that?' I replied that I thought the Lord had revealed it to me. He told me that, when he was a child growing up, his parents said to him, 'If you do not pass your examinations we will not love you.' Can you imagine any parent saying that? Now, what happens when a child grows up in an atmosphere of conditional love? You show me a child who is brought up in that atmosphere and I will show you a child who is hurt, because children's hearts are designed and created by God to be loved. But all he was receiving was conditional love: *if* you do that then we will love you. So as he grows up and goes to university, he is away from home but in his heart there is resentment and bitterness and hostility towards his parents.

All that was going on deep down inside him, and he wasn't the kind of man that could go to his parents and say, 'Look, Mum and Dad, you have hurt me by giving me conditional love. I don't want to hold hostility towards you. Let's have this thing out. Let me show you what it has meant to me and how it has hurt me so much.' He didn't have the strength or the courage to confront them in that way so he allowed the pool of bitterness and poison to remain in his heart. His real desire was to get back at his parents, and what better way to retaliate than to fail in his examinations, because that would upset them more than anything. Now, you tell me: was he failing or was he succeeding? Yes, he was succeeding, because he was getting what he was *really* willing deep down.

You know, my prayer life has undergone a revolution since my contact with Temple's book, *Nature, Man and God*, because it brought me face to face with the fact that much of my prayer life was egocentric. I look back to the early days of my Christian life as a pastor and my heart is ashamed as so many of the things that I did and said were done as a covert bid for attention. So often I would pray high-sounding prayers, asking with the fruit of my lips for God to be glorified, but actually, deep down in my heart, and I say this shamefacedly, it was my own glory that I was really wanting. I asked for things that sounded deeply spiritual and important, but behind them was that covert bid for attention.

What Archbishop Temple suggests is that if you are not receiving at a certain level when you ask, then go to another level and examine your heart. Ask: is this what I really want? This is what I do now when I pray, and I find that so much of my spiritual life, my prayer life, is quite different from what it used to be. Instead of asking for things, I spend my time asking: do I really want this? It is so easy to come to God with the fruit of our lips and say all the right things, but what do we really want, deep down in our hearts?

So, may I remind you again, if your spiritual life is not as full as it ought to be and you are not receiving all the things that God wants you to receive, *the fault is not in God*. His magnanimity knows no bounds. Jesus has cleared away the mists and misconceptions around the character of God: God longs to bless His children and delights in it. So it is never *His* fault if you are not receiving. Jesus, I think, is saying: look at your own heart, examine your concept of God. Ask yourself: am I merely wanting it, wishing for it, or is my true willing in God's direction? And when your willing comes in line with God's eagerness to give, when those two match up, then nothing is impossible. Or as Archbishop William Temple puts it: 'you will receive as much as you will for and as little as you are satisfied with.'

Let us end with this prayer:

PRAYER

O God, we pray that You will help us to examine our hearts until our eagerness to receive matches Your willingness to give. And grant that we may remove from our hearts any distortions or misconceptions that we have about You. Help us to see that You really like to give, that it's the joy of Your heart to give to Your children. And grant that Your eagerness to give might be matched by our eagerness to receive. In Jesus' name. Amen.

5

THE
FOUR DIMENSIONS
OF GOD'S LOVE

JOHN 3:16; EPHESIANS 3:18

For God so loved the world, that he gave his only begotten Son, that whosoever believeth in him should not perish, but have everlasting life.

John 3:16, AV

... may have power, together with all the saints, to grasp how wide and long and high and deep is the love of Christ ...

Ephesians 3:18

This first text is arguably the greatest text in the whole of the Bible. It is, to my mind, the world's most powerful text in the world's most powerful book, and I am sure you know it so well. I am joining this text to a second, from the book of Ephesians, because sometimes in the Bible, when you marry two texts together, one brings out the flavour of the other. And sometimes, when you put one scripture against another, they seem to answer each other and echo some of the things that each one is saying. One brings out the hidden meaning of the other.

So my second text is Ephesians 3:18. Paul prays that we might understand what is the depth and the length and the breadth and the height of the love of Christ. Now everywhere in the New Testament Paul is always trying to measure the love of God, but how can you measure the immeasurable? How can you define the indefinable? How can you exhaust the inexhaustible? It is impossible to measure the love of God, the marvellous, wonderful, fantastic, glorious love of God! So, how can we comprehend it?

Read John 3:16 again and see that this text is the centre of gravity of the Bible. All the Old Testament truths converge upon it and all the New Testament truths emerge from it. It is at the heart of the evangel, the hub of the gospel. If I only had one text and all the Bibles in the world were destroyed, there is enough power in John 3:16 for me to go around the world and preach the gospel of our Lord Jesus Christ. It is God's greatest word ever. Paul was praying that we might comprehend what is the breadth of God's love. How can we measure the breadth of God's love? Here's the answer: *for God so loved the world.* That's how broad God's love is.

When the first men went to the moon and turned the cameras onto Earth, as some of you may have seen on television, what a spectacle that was, this shining orb, this marvellous Earth! No one had ever seen it before the cameras in space. And when the cameras were turned onto Earth, Billy Graham was in his living room watching. He went over to the television set, put his arms around it and hugged the world to himself. That is the heart of an evangelist. That's what an evangelist does, and I am an evangelist as well as a Bible teacher, and one of the most exciting things about the gospel of Jesus Christ is this: that God loved not just one country, not just one race, not just one people, not just one part of this world but, when the world fell and Adam and Eve sinned, God ran after us and put His arms around the five continents and the seven seas and drew this world to Himself. So good is God's love!

God takes in the British and the Americans and the Asians and the Africans ... every single race, every man and woman born in this world. God loves us so much! That's how broad His love is. When the angels fell from heaven, there was no hand outstretched to save. God let them fall.

That's what the Bible teaches. The angels fell because they sinned. But, when mankind sinned, God put His arms around the continents and drew them to Himself. The hymnist Frederick M. Lehman said this:

> Could we with ink the ocean fill,
> and were the skies of parchment made,
> were every stalk on earth a quill,
> and every man a scribe by trade,
> to write the love of God above,
> would drain the ocean dry;
> nor could the scroll contain the whole,
> though stretched from sky to sky.

There is no real way to describe the love of God, and Paul's prayer suggests that it is not something any one of us on our own can comprehend. Rather, it takes all the saints together to comprehend it even feebly. Then we begin to come close to comprehending how broad is the love of God!

So we know how broad God's love is, but how long is it? If the breadth of God's love is that He so loved the world, then how *long* is His love? The answer is: 'that he gave his only begotten Son'. Now the Bible never says that God gave anybody until He gave Jesus. He sent Moses, He sent David, He sent Elijah, He sent the great prophets but He never gave them, until one day, up there in heaven, God saw you and me and the plight we were in because of sin. And so long is His love that He will go to the greatest lengths possible to save us. And that is what He did when He gave His only Son. He went to the furthest limits.

Many years ago when I was a pastor, as I was for eighteen years, I made a terrible mistake. I was only a young pastor and it is easy to make mistakes when you are young. As you get older people expect you not to make so many. So, I was just a young pastor, and a man, a wealthy businessman, gave a lot of money to the church. I said to him, 'What you have given is a great sum but it doesn't really cost you very much because you still have a lot more money left in your bank account and all that has really happened is that the bank clerks have changed the figures in your account and really you haven't felt any pain giving this money.' And of course he looked at me in amazement and he almost left the church because of that. That was a foolish thing to say. But the point that I wanted to make was that love is not just measured by what it is, but also by its costliness. When God gave His only Son He had no other son left. He gave the only one He had in order that you and I might be saved and converted. Years later, I was down on the equator in Kisumu in Kenya where I have a friend, a chief by the name of Silas Owitti. One day he said to me, 'Look at this.' Taking out his guitar he began to play and sing a song to me in the East African language of Kikuyu and, when he translated it into English, they were some of the most beautiful lines that I had ever heard:

> There's a limit to the number of the wondrous stars that shine,
> There's a limit to the wealth of gold that is in every mine,
> There's a limit to the number of trees in every glade,
> There's a limit to the number of blades of grass that He made,
> But I know when I gaze upon Calvary
> that there isn't any limit to His love for me.

You see, there is no limit to the length to which God will go to save us – no boundaries, no barriers. Some of you may be surveyors or accountants, but you will never be able to estimate or evaluate the love of Christ. Bring all your accountancy books, bring all your computers, bring all your diagrams, bring all your plans! The love of God beggars description, defies analysis, leaps over any attempts to describe it, and the only way that we can begin to comprehend it is to recognise that God's love is so long that He gave His only begotten Son.

And how deep is it? We know what the breadth of God's love is: *'for God so loved the world'*; we know how long it is: *'that he gave his only begotten Son'* – now how *deep* is it? Note this: *'that whosoever believeth in him should not perish'*. Whosoever? What does that mean? You know, I am glad it says *whosoever* because, if it said my name there – if it said 'for God so loved the world that Selwyn Hughes who believes in Him should not perish' – it wouldn't be half so exciting. And do you know why? Because there are many in Wales who go by the name of Selwyn Hughes! And the devil would come to me and say, 'It doesn't mean you, it means another Selwyn Hughes.' But, you see, the word 'whosoever' means *everybody*. We are all included.

I remember talking one day to some children and I wanted to point out to them what the word 'whosoever' meant. So this is what I did. I walked to the table at the front of the church and, without anyone seeing what I was doing, I slipped under a cup a very large British coin. It was called half a crown in those days, which was quite a lot of money to give to a child. As I put the money under the cup I shouted to the children, 'Whosoever will come and take what is under this cup can have it!' And all the children rushed up and then I stood in front of them and said, 'Did I call you by name?' And they all looked very sheepish and shamefaced and turned and went back to their seats. But there was one little boy who just stood there, and I said to him,

'What are you doing here?'

He said, 'I want what is under the cup, sir.'

And I said, 'Did I call you by name?'

'No, sir.'

'Then what are you doing here?'

'I want what is under the cup, sir.'

'Listen to me. Did I call you by name?' And I looked very sternly at him. But he stood his ground and I said again, 'Why are you here?'

'I want what is under the cup, sir.'

'Now let me ask you one more time. Did I call you by name?'

'No, sir.'

'Then why are you here?'

He replied, 'You said "whosoever", and that means me!'

That is the wonder of the gospel: whosoever means anybody. If *your* name were there, the devil would say, 'It doesn't mean you. It means somebody else.' This is how deep God's love is: *'that whosoever believeth in him should not perish'.*

Do you know what it means to believe? It means to put your whole trust in, put all your weight on, somebody. That's what I did as a young man in Wales many years ago. I put my weight on Jesus Christ and I trusted Him to become my Saviour and He saved me and changed my life and I have now been in the ministry, preaching the gospel of Jesus Christ around the world, for fifty years. You see, what it means to believe is this: to trust Jesus by putting your weight on Him.

I am sure you have heard of the great tightrope walker Blondin who lived in the USA many years ago. He used to walk across wires placed at great heights, and one day he decided to string a wire across the Niagara Falls, which has one of its banks in Canada and the other in America. Thousands of people came to watch him walk across the wire, knowing that if he fell it would be into the raging torrent of the Niagara. Among those watching him was a little boy, no doubt with his mouth wide open and his eyes popping in his head. 'That's fantastic!' he said to his mother. 'Look at him walking across that rope! If he slips he will fall to his death!'

Climbing down the ladder after walking the tightrope, Blondin saw the little boy gazing at him in awe and, walking over to him, he said, 'Did you see what I did?'

The little boy gasped, 'Ah, yes, sir! That was fantastic! That was wonderful!'

Then Blondin said, 'Do you believe that I can take a wheelbarrow and wheel it across that rope?'

The little boy said, 'Yes, sir!' He was willing to believe anything after seeing this feat with his own eyes. 'Yes, sir. I sure believe you could do that.'

So Blondin took a wheelbarrow right up the ladder, wheeled it across the Falls, came back down the ladder again and asked the boy what he thought of this. 'I thought you were going to fall, sir,' said the little boy, 'and you didn't. It was marvellous!'

'Do you believe that I could carry you across in that wheelbarrow?' said Blondin.

'Oh, yes, sir,' he replied. 'Sure, sir!'

'Well get in,' said Blondin.

'No fear!' said the little boy.

Just so, there are many people who are willing to *believe* that Jesus Christ can bring them to heaven but they are not willing to *trust* Him. They have never surrendered their lives to Him, never given Him their hearts.

Consider again: '*whosoever believes in Him should not perish*'.

However bad you are, whatever sins you have committed, if you come to Jesus He can forgive your sins and change you. He will write your name in the Lamb's book of life in heaven, He will cleanse you with His blood and He will make you into a new person. You will be a new person if you surrender your life to Jesus Christ.

We ask now: What is the *height* of God's love? The breadth of God's love is that *'He so loved the world'*; the length of His love is that *'He gave His only begotten Son'*; the depth of His love is that *'whosoever believeth in Him should not perish'*. The height of His love is that they shall *'have everlasting life.'*

Let me ask you a question: Have you got everlasting life? Now you don't need to have passed an examination to answer that question and it doesn't matter what kind of education you have had. Anyone can answer that question: Have you got everlasting life? Have you received Jesus Christ into your heart as your personal Saviour? Because, you see, 2,000 years ago, on the cross, Jesus Christ died to take away our sins. In order to appropriate that and make it meaningful in our lives we must receive Him into our hearts as our personal Lord and Saviour. And why did He die on that cross? Why do we have crosses in our churches? Why do we have crosses over our churches? Why do we wear crosses around our necks? Because, on the cross, something happened that means that every sin we have ever committed can be forgiven. Jesus said in the Garden of Gethsemane, as He moved towards the cross, that there were twelve legions of angels that His Father could put at His disposal to save Him from the cross (Matt. 26:53–54). One legion of Roman soldiers is 6,000, so that means 72,000 angels would have pulled their swords and rescued Jesus from the cross. But God said, 'No, let Him die.' Why? Because, in that moment, God looked down the telescope of time and saw you, and it was for you that Jesus came to die. And if you have never received Him into your life then you don't have eternal life. If you have never opened your heart to Him, if you have never come to Christ, if you have never submitted yourself to Him, then you will be lost. That is what Scripture teaches. To avoid perishing, you open your life to receive Jesus and, when you do receive Him, you have life. So, if you die today, you go straight into heaven into the presence of God!

Now, let us consider again, finally, how to comprehend the breadth, the length, the depth and the height of the love of Christ. How broad is it? He took in the whole world. How long? He gave His only begotten Son. How deep? That whosoever believes in Him should not perish. And how high? They shall have everlasting life.

The question I want to end with is this: Have you got everlasting life? Are you sure? Are you sure that you have invited Jesus into your life? Do you know the Lord Jesus Christ in a personal way? I am not talking about a religion, I am talking about a relationship. Have you got a personal relationship with Jesus?

If you don't know Jesus as your Saviour and Lord, open yourself to Him now and receive Him into your heart and life. And if you haven't and you are saying in your heart, 'I want to receive Jesus Christ into my heart and my life as my Saviour and Lord', close your eyes now and pray this prayer:

PRAYER

Lord Jesus, I come to You right here and now and I open my life to You. I receive Jesus Christ into my life as my Lord and Saviour. Wash away my sins. Write my name in Your book in heaven, and help me to be a good Christian. Save me, Lord Jesus, wash away my stains and give me that assurance that today, right here, I met Jesus Christ and opened my life to Him. In Jesus' name. Amen.

God bless you.

6

THE DEMANDS
OF DISCIPLESHIP

LUKE 14:25–33

Large crowds were travelling with Jesus, and turning to them he said: 'If anyone comes to me and does not hate his father and mother, his wife and children, his brothers and sisters – yes, even his own life – he cannot be my disciple. And anyone who does not carry his cross and follow me cannot be my disciple.

'Suppose one of you wants to build a tower. Will he not first sit down and estimate the cost to see if he has enough money to complete it? For if he lays the foundation and is not able to finish it, everyone who sees it will ridicule him, saying, "This fellow began to build and was not able to finish."

'Or suppose a king is about to go to war against another king. Will he not first sit down and consider whether he is able with ten thousand men to oppose the one coming against him with twenty thousand? If he is not able, he will send a delegation while the other is still a long way off and will ask for terms of peace. In the same way, any of you who does not give up everything he has cannot be my disciple.'

Some years ago, Sir David McNee, a Christian and Chief Commissioner of the London Metropolitan Police, was addressing a group of ministers, of which I was one, at High Leigh Conference Centre in England. He spoke about one of the tests given to candidates for selection as police cadets. This is the scenario they were asked to imagine:

One afternoon you are patrolling your beat in a busy London suburb when suddenly a gas main explodes in the middle of the road creating a huge crater that makes it impossible for the traffic to proceed in any direction. A number of vehicles collide with one another and you go to help a lady driver who appears to be in distress only to find that she is the wife of your local police inspector and her breath is reeking of alcohol. As this happens, a man comes running out of a shop doorway and informs you that, due to the explosion, his eight-month pregnant wife has gone into labour and he asks for your help in calling for an ambulance. At this point the gas main ignites, sending flames high into the air and causing people to run away from the scene, and in the rush several people are injured. One of the men running from the scene you recognise as a wanted criminal whose photograph has been on display in the police station. Immediately you see this, two dogs start fighting in the middle of the road and you notice that neither of them has a collar, which is an offence in Britain. Now hundreds of people begin shouting at you to do something.

How would you proceed to bring things under control?

According to Sir David, one policeman said, 'I would slip out of my uniform and get lost in the crowd.' He failed the test!

Now I want to put before you a different kind of test, a more biblical one. It is a test that Jesus gave to certain of His followers two thousand years ago and, believe me, it is still as applicable today as it was then. I call it the test of discipleship. We have already read about it in Luke chapter 14.

Let me ask you, 'What do you think is the biggest issue facing the

Church today?' I know there will be many different opinions and for some of you the biggest issue, perhaps, will be church growth. Well, that may be so. Or some might say that it is demonology, and others that it is evangelism. It's a question to which there can be a variety of answers, as we all have different ideas about what should be the main item on the Church's agenda. But let me tell you what I think: the item that is top of God's agenda today is *discipleship*. That, I believe, is what God is concerned about in the hour in which we are living. He wants to know whether we are His disciples or not.

I really believe that the Church of Jesus Christ is desperately in need of a new definition of discipleship. The word has become so smudged and discoloured over years of misuse that we really need once again to redefine just what it means to be a disciple. You see, when we look at the Early Church, we find a tremendous difference between the Church of that day and the Church of this day. One difference is that today, generally speaking, we will preach 3,000 sermons to get one person converted, while on the day of Pentecost they preached one sermon and 3,000 people were converted. Doesn't that highlight the difference between the Church of the first century and the Church of today?

The Early Church was powerful. Today, we are seldom bold enough to give advice. We tiptoe our way through things, afraid of bringing the denunciation of the world upon us. And, let me tell you, the world, by and large, is not impressed with the brand of discipleship of modern-day Christianity. There are exceptions to what I am saying, of course, and your experience may be an exception. If so, that is good. But I believe with all my heart that what the Christian Church needs is a new vision of what it means to be a disciple of the Lord Jesus Christ.

Now what is a disciple? The word 'disciple' occurs 260 times in the New Testament and it actually pre-dates the word 'Christian'. People were called disciples before they were called Christians. A disciple, you see, is a follower, a learner, an imbiber, an assimilator, someone who follows the master step by step, moment by moment, fully committed, fully determined to follow his master all the way. I want to ask you a question that is well within the capability of every person, young or old, to answer. Answering it may transform your life. This could be a watershed day in your experience. My question to you is: are you a disciple?

I am not asking you: are you a Christian? The reason is that you can be a Christian, and you can go through life and make it to heaven by the grace of God and yet miss the real issue of discipleship. Jesus gives us a test in Luke 14 and I want to put this before you and then ask you whether you can say, 'I am a disciple.'

Listen to what Jesus says first of all: He says that we must hate our father and our mother. Let me quote the words to you: 'If anyone comes to me and does not hate his father and mother, his wife and children, his brothers and sisters – yes, even his own life – he cannot be my disciple.'

Let me tell you quite frankly that when I was a young Christian that verse put me right off. It almost put me off Christianity because I said to myself, 'There is no way that I am going to hate my father and mother!' But this is one of the hard sayings of Jesus that many people misunderstand because what Jesus is actually saying here is not that we suddenly turn in hatred from our parents but that we must not *prefer* them, put them before Him.

You only have to look at Paul's first letter to Timothy to read: 'But if anyone does not provide for his own, and especially for those of his household, he has denied the faith and is worse than an unbeliever' (1 Tim. 5:8, NKJV).

The whole tenor of the New Testament is that of love and care for family. It is also one of the Ten Commandments that we honour our father and mother. As always, when we come to interpret Scripture we must use what is clear to interpret what is unclear and, undeniably, Scripture as a whole teaches that we must love our parents. So what Jesus is saying here, and He actually uses this word elsewhere in the New Testament, is that we must not *prefer* them, that is, put them before Him.

And so, here is the first test of discipleship: that we put Jesus Christ first and foremost before every other person in our lives.

Committing our lives to Jesus Christ automatically affects, cuts into, every other relationship that we have. The question of whom to marry, for instance, takes on a new solemnity when you are a disciple of Jesus Christ. Suddenly a huge question mark arises about the people to whom we relate because He says that being His disciple means putting Him first and foremost before every other person in our lives. There must be a willingness to put Christ first and others second.

Now it is important to understand that there is a reason why Jesus raises the standard to these almost unbelievable heights. The Church is suffering today from what I call 'easy believe-ism' because, at some evangelistic services, people are introduced to Christ in strange ways. People are told, 'Sign this card and say this prayer, then you will have forgiveness of sins and you will be able to sit down at the marriage supper of the Lamb. You will have a mansion in the heavens, a diamond-studded crown and you will be in charge of five cities in the millennium.' But, when Jesus came He rigorously challenged people. Time and time again, He would work miracle after miracle and then, when He had worked the miracle and people wanted to applaud Him, He would prick the bubble of applause with astonishing messages saying, in effect, 'Now I have got your attention through miracles, *this* is what it means to be my disciple.' And, on one occasion related in John 6, hundreds of them turned away and that is why He turned to His own disciples and said, 'Will you also go away?' (vv.66–67). You see, Jesus raises the standard to almost unbelievable heights and He calls people to a radical commitment to Him, not a wishy-washy kind of Christianity where you take Him on today and then maybe forget all about Him tomorrow. What Christ is looking for is a new brand of disciple who will stand for Him, raise the standard and say, 'I am on His side and He is first and foremost in my life!'

Now, if we don't preach that in our evangelism, people are going to slip into the kingdom of God without this radical commitment to Christ and they are going to be arguing with Him all the way through their Christian lives. I know many people who have never experienced a radical conversion in the sense of making a deep-down commitment, and when they come into the Christian Church, what happens is that they argue and remonstrate with Christ on almost every issue. This is why Jesus came preaching *repentance* and this is why He told His Church to preach repentance. If people do not repent when they come into the Christian life then they become insubordinate, endlessly arguing with God. But, if they come in through radical repentance, their will capitulates, their ego surrenders before the cross and they serve Jesus without argument.

Actually, you can't argue with Christ. At least, you can argue with Him but you will lose the argument every time because He is right on every issue, never makes a mistake, never says anything wrong. I am afraid that much of our evangelism today is really 'evan*jelly*ism'. It has no real ring of radical commitment to it and people are encouraged to come into the kingdom of God in a half-hearted kind of way. But Jesus never watered down or sugar-coated His message. He knew that people needed to make a radical commitment. And do you know what this kind of evan*jelly*ism produces in the Christian Church? Evan*jellybabies*!

To be a disciple of Jesus Christ means to be willing to put Christ first and foremost before every other person in your life.

One of the sad things happening in our age is that, in the pulpits of many churches, we hear preachers who drip like a November fog, offering no real challenge to the men and women of their day. Many preachers today are just tearing pages out of the Bible, saying they don't believe this and they don't believe that.

I know a dear old lady, a committed Christian, who attended a church in Cardiff, South Wales, where the liberal minister kept saying, 'Well, I am not sure that this is in the original. Maybe you ought to tear that page out of your Bible because I am not certain that it is inspired.' He kept saying this throughout the two- or three-year period of his ministry. Then, one day he went to visit the old lady when she had been very sick, and he asked her if she would like him to pray for her and if she had a Bible. 'Oh yes, I have got my Bible,' she said. 'I was reading it before you came and I think your prayer ought to be for healing.'

'Why do you think that?' he asked.

'It says in Mark 16 that they shall lay hands on the sick and they shall recover,' she answered.

'Oh, my dear,' said the minister, 'in what part of Mark 16 is that?'

'In the last part,' she said.

'That's not in the original,' said he, 'it's not in the original at all. People have written that in afterwards.'

'Praise the Lord! Hallelujah!' she cried.

And he, astonished, asked, 'What do you mean?'

'Well,' she said, 'when I was reading this before you came, I suddenly began to realise that God could heal me and, as I read those words and prayed, something happened to me and His healing power came into my body!'

'Are you sure?' he asked. 'Are you sure?'

'Oh yes!' she said.

'Then why are you so excited about what I have just said?' he asked.

'Well,' she said, 'if the Lord can heal me through something that is not in the original, what about the rest of it that is?'

So, let me ask you again, 'Can you pass that first test? Are you willing to put Christ first and foremost *before every other person in your life?*' That is the first test of discipleship and that's the brand of discipleship that Christ is looking for in these days.

Now let's consider a second test of discipleship which we find in this text:

> Then Jesus said to his disciples, 'If anyone would come after me, he must deny himself and take up his cross and follow me.'
>
> Matt. 16:24

What does it mean to take up a cross? Do you know, I find Christians are confused about this. It is amazing how many people misunderstand what Jesus is saying here. Let me tell you first of all what it does *not* mean. The cross does not mean the unavoidable irritations of life, as in the case of the man John Wesley mentions in one of his journals who said that his cross was a smoking chimney. It does not mean the people we find difficult to cope with, nor does it, as some people think, mean the unavoidable sufferings of life. These are all wrong ideas about the cross that we are to take up.

A doctor once said to me that many of the sicknesses he sees in his patients are really the involuntary confessions of their own guilt – a kind of atoning for it. The guilt we feel inside has to be settled somehow and, very often what happens, unconsciously, is that we try to pay it ourselves. We actually bring sickness upon ourselves and, in a sense, the sicker we feel the better we feel.

I once knew a woman who worked full-time in Christian ministry and was riddled with guilt, not real guilt, but imaginary, or pseudo, guilt that made her suffer sickness. Sickness was for her, she came to understand, a way of dealing with these guilty feelings and achieving a sense that God was pleased with her. What these examples point to is a truth that guilt is something that demands payment because God has written His character into the whole of the universe. And you either make payment yourself or you make others pay. The alternative God gives us is to bring the guilt to the cross where Christ has paid the penalty for it all.

I remember a man some years ago telling me that he suffered for Christ and, when I asked how he suffered, he said, 'All my neighbours are against me and avoid me.'

'Why?' I asked.

He said, 'Because I've talked to them about Christ.'

What he was actually saying to them, I discovered, was, 'Do you know you are going to hell?' It is one thing when people hate us because of Christ, but it is another thing when they hate Christ because of us.

So, by commanding us to take up our cross, Jesus is not talking about the unavoidable sufferings of life, nor is He saying that He wants us to suffer in some way physically. And nor does He have in mind the irritation, aggravation and frustration we experience in life. Let me ask you if you know how these three things differ from each other, and illustrate the difference for you.

A group of students were sitting around one night and one young man wanted to play a game. About midnight, he picked a number from the phone book and rang it. When a weary-sounding voice answered he asked, 'Is Sam there?'

'No. There isn't anyone by the name of Sam here and it is midnight. You should be careful about who you call at this time of night!' The phone was slammed down.

Turning to his friends the young man said, 'Now that's irritation.'

An hour later he said, 'I will demonstrate to you what aggravation is,' and he dialled the same number again and asked the same question.

'No!' responded the sleepy voice. 'I told you an hour ago: Sam does not live here and you have woken me up.' Again the phone was slammed down.

'That,' he said to his friends, 'is aggravation.' At 3am he said, 'Now I will show you frustration,' and he redialled the number. When the phone was picked up, he said, 'This is Sam. Have there been any messages for me in the last few hours?'

We all experience irritation, aggravation and frustration at times, but we are not to call them a cross because these experiences in life are often unavoidable.

The cross is something you can avoid; it is something you choose to pick up. The cross that Jesus is talking about is that point at which our self-interest and our self-concern intersect with His will and with His demands. Visualise now, if you will, with your mind's eye, a perpendicular line, running perfectly straight before you. Then imagine a horizontal line cutting right across the middle of it. At the point where the horizontal line intersects with the vertical line a cross appears, and that is what Jesus is talking about when He says, 'Take up your cross.' What Jesus is asking is, 'Are you willing to put your self-concern and your self-interest to one side and to make my cause and my claims a priority?'

The test of discipleship is not only that you will put Christ first and foremost before every person in your life but also, secondly, that you will put Him first and foremost before every *pleasure* in your life. Are you willing to take up that cross? Because I tell you this: the commands and claims of Jesus Christ will sometimes intersect with your own demands and desires. Are you willing at that stage to say, 'He comes first'?

There is within all of us, and I sense it in my own life, after more than fifty years in the ministry, an awful stubbornness that makes us continue the struggle to have our own way. When I am reading my Bible nowadays, I sometimes hear God speaking to me and I find something coming up in my heart that makes me respond, 'I don't want to do that.' Do you find that or are you more spiritual than I am? Don't you find sometimes, when you come up against the commands and claims of Jesus Christ, that you really don't want to go His way? And then, when you bring this feeling into submission and obedience to Him, that's when that cross appears. It means willingly, submissively, saying to yourself, 'God's demands come first, before every other pleasure in my life.' That place, where the desires of our own life intersect with the will of God, is where a cross appears. It is something you can avoid, as you may not be able to avoid some sickness, some suffering or irritation. It is something you can choose either to ignore or take up. It is a willing commitment.

To be a disciple of Jesus Christ means the acceptance of personal discipline, the discipline of spending time with Him in prayer and in the Word of God. Jesus delighted to do the will of His Father. The greatest challenge that I have in my life is what I do with my time. And it seems to me that all the issues of discipleship can almost be narrowed down to that one single thing – what do I do with my time? Because, if Jesus Christ is first and foremost in my life, then it means that He has a claim on every minute of my time. That doesn't mean that He is going to demand that I do this and that and never give me time for any leisure. I don't want to go in the direction of legalism, which is a road the Church has gone down too often. No, Jesus is saying, 'If you really want to be My disciple, My claims must control your time, the films that you see, the things that you watch, the way that you use your talents, the way that you discipline your life. If you want to be My disciple, you must put Me first and foremost, before every pleasure in your life.'

And then this is His third test, He says, '... any of you who does not give up everything he has cannot be my disciple.' Jesus is talking here about possessions, and is clearly saying, 'If you are not prepared to pass this test, then call yourself a Christian but don't call yourself My disciple.' I love that word 'disciple' because it was the word Jesus used. It means putting Christ first and foremost before every other person, before every other pleasure and before *every other possession*. He that does not forsake all that he has cannot be a disciple of Jesus. Do you call your possessions your own? Does the Lord have access to your bank account? Maybe He can have everything or, as one person said to me some years ago, 'He can have everything except my money.' There was a young man like this in the New Testament, referred to as 'the rich young ruler'. He was mightily interested in Jesus Christ but, when Jesus probed that area of his possessions, he turned away and went down into oblivion (see Matt. 19:16–30).

The great hymn *Guide me O Thou great Jehovah, pilgrim through this barren land*, was written first of all in Welsh. When it was first translated into English the words 'land me safe on Canaan's side' were translated 'land my safe on Canaan's side'. Isn't that what a lot of Christians would like? They would like to take their money with them when they die, but let me ask you: 'Have you ever seen a trailer behind a hearse?' It can't be done, can it?

What Jesus is saying is that, if you really want to follow Him and be His disciple, then you must be ready and willing to give Him all that He is asking – and He is asking for *all*. As someone said, 'If you do not crown Him Lord of all you do not crown Him Lord at all'. And, if He is worthy of our commitment, then it must be a radical, wholehearted, 100 per cent commitment. C.T. Studd, the great missionary, said, 'If Jesus Christ be God and died for me, then no sacrifice can be too great for me to make for Him'. And our money is usually the last thing to be laid upon the altar.

There is a true story about a farmer in West Wales who had one hundred cows. Along with a lot of farmers, he attended an apostolic church. One Sunday morning the preacher took as his theme giving our possessions to God, and talked specifically about tithing. 'What tithing means', he said, 'is that if you have got one hundred cows then you give ten to the Lord'. There was one young farmer in the congregation who had a real problem with giving money, but when he heard the preacher say this, he said 'Amen', because he didn't possess one hundred cows. Then the preacher went on to say, 'Now, if you have fifty cows, it means you give five to the Lord'. And the man said, 'Amen', because he didn't have fifty cows. And he said 'Amen' again when the preacher said, 'If you have twenty cows, you give two to the Lord'. But when the preacher came down to ten cows and said, 'This means you give one to the Lord', the young farmer leapt up and said, 'Now, come on, preacher, you know I have ten cows!'

Why does Jesus make these demands – for that is what they are – the demands of discipleship? Why does He make them so strong? I will tell you.

Let's consider again the text:

'Suppose one of you wants to build a tower. Will he not first sit down and estimate the cost to see if he has enough money to complete it? For if he lays the foundation and is not able to finish it, everyone who sees it will ridicule him, saying, "This fellow began to build and was not able to finish."

'Or suppose a king is about to go to war against another king. Will he not first sit down and consider whether he is able with ten thousand men to oppose the one coming against him with twenty thousand?'

The usual interpretation of this passage is that that before you become a disciple of Jesus Christ you must sit down and count the cost. That is not the right interpretation. Jesus is not saying that before you become His disciple you should reckon up whether you can really pay the cost, because the message of Jesus Christ is always this – come at all cost. You are going to be the loser if you don't come. What Jesus is actually doing here is illustrating that someone, before beginning to build a tower or going to war, sits down to count the cost, and that this is exactly what He Himself is doing. He is saying, 'I am in the world to build, I am in the world to overturn its systems, I am here to change and challenge the world and, in order to do it, I want to be absolutely certain that the people who come to me are totally committed and totally dedicated.' He is the one who is counting the cost and He is making it absolutely clear that, if He is to change the world, if He is to lay hold upon men and women and lay siege to the stubborn and recalcitrant hearts of the nations of the world, then He is thinking very carefully about the breed and the brand of people that He wants to follow Him. He is saying, 'Now here are my commands. Here is my standard. This is what I am asking for.'

So, to reiterate, there are three tests of discipleship: Are you willing to put Christ first and foremost before every other *person* in your life, every other *pleasure*, every other *possession?* Somebody said that the stages of the Christian life could be described in four words: easy, hard, difficult, impossible. Some people think that it is easy to be a Christian: all you have to do is sign on the dotted line, say a prayer and you are in. When they get in, they find that it is a little harder than they thought. And then they go through a phase where it is extremely difficult and, finally, they come to a stage where it is impossible. When they come to this final stage they are at the point of their greatest breakthrough, because, actually, you cannot live this life in your own strength. There is no way that you can be a disciple of Christ by your own energy entirely. You become a disciple by committing yourself to Him.

My friend, are you a disciple of Christ? Do you drift and dawdle and go in and out of Christian fellowship? Is your Christian life shaky and lacking real dedication and commitment to Jesus Christ? Then I am going to ask you here and now to make a radical commitment. And I am not asking you, 'Are you a Christian?' but 'Are you a disciple of Jesus?' Are you ready to take your place with that breed and brand of disciple that Jesus is asking for in this generation? Are you willing to redefine discipleship so that it means something so radical that the Church can stand in the midst of a pagan society and show the world that twenty-first-century discipleship is similar to first-century discipleship? That's what the world is crying out for. And, believe me, the world needs disciples, perhaps more than it needs a cure for cancer – and it needs that badly enough. Perhaps the greatest need of the Church at this moment is for disciples.

Let me take you back to the coronation of Queen Elizabeth II in Westminster Abbey, London in 1953. Back to a marvellous moment, a very moving and dramatic moment, which you may have seen on television or pictured elsewhere, when she was just about to be crowned. The Archbishop of Canterbury, the chief citizen of the realm who plays a leading role in this drama, comes with great reverence before Elizabeth. Holding the crown so high above the head of the soon-to-be Queen that every eye in the Abbey can see what is taking place, he utters these words in a voice that resounds down the nave to every part of the building: 'I present unto you Elizabeth, the undoubted queen of the realm! Are you willing to do her homage?' And it is not until an answering shout of affirmation rings through the Abbey that the crown is placed on her head.

So I present unto you Jesus Christ, the undoubted Lord of the universe. Are you willing to do Him homage?

I am asking you whether you want to commit yourself now to Jesus Christ, to be His disciple. Maybe you have been a half-hearted Christian, lacking in dedication and commitment, but God can turn you into a flaming brand of fire in His kingdom. He is looking for *real* disciples and, if you have come to feel that the test of discipleship is something you can't pass, then that is good, because as you realise that it is impossible to do in your own strength, you are in the place to make the greatest breakthrough of your life. You have to realise that you can't do it in your own strength and come and stand humbly before Him.

What you are asking God to give you now is a new brand of discipleship, not just to be a Christian, wonderful as that is, but a true disciple of Jesus. As you pray this prayer, really put your heart in God's hands and just surrender to Him:

PRAYER

Lord Jesus, I come to You now with all my weakness and with all my emptiness. I give my life into Your hands. I want to be a disciple, totally committed to You. Take me now, Lord, as I put You first and foremost before every other person, every other pleasure, every other possession. You are mine and I am Yours. I put myself in Your hands. Now fill me with Your Spirit from the crown of my head to the soles of my feet so that every part of me shall be Yours, indwelt by You, dominated by You. You are my Lord and I give You all the praise and all the honour and all the glory. Amen.

~ 7 ~
THE CHRIST
OF BURNING,
CLEANSING FLAME

MATTHEW 3:11

'I baptise you with water for repentance. But after me will come one who is more powerful than I, whose sandals I am not fit to carry. He will baptise you with the Holy Spirit and with fire. His winnowing fork is in his hand, and he will clear his threshing-floor, gathering his wheat into the barn and burning up the chaff with unquenchable fire.'

I want you to come back with me in your imagination to one of the most momentous meetings in history – the meeting between Jesus and John the Baptist as recorded in the passage above. It took place long before there were any denominations: no Anglicans, no Methodists, no Presbyterians, no Pentecostals, no Charismatics. There was just one Baptist!

What a moment it is! John and Jesus are standing at the dividing line of the centuries. The old dispensation is about to come to an end and a new one begin. And what an age it had been. In Old Testament times miracles and supernatural events were the order of the day. Seas had parted, manna came down from heaven, supernatural fire illuminated the path of the Israelites sometimes as they made their way through the wilderness at dead of night. And think of this: Moses, the great leader of the children of Israel, climbed to the top of Mount Sinai and there witnessed the hand of God inscribing on tablets of stone in His own handwriting the Ten Commandments.

Move on a few books of the Bible and you come to the prophet Elijah who seemed to be surrounded by the supernatural. Wherever he goes astonishing things happen; miracle after miracle takes place in his ministry, and when he gets ready to go to heaven God sends down a chariot of fire and horses to take him home to glory. I remember, as a boy, asking my father, who was a local preacher, why God sent down horses and a chariot of fire to take Elijah to heaven, and his answer was: 'Elijah was such a red-hot prophet that God didn't want him to get cold on the way up.'

Now the Old Testament age was about to pass away and a new one begin – inaugurated, of course, by none other than Jesus Christ Himself. I have often pondered on whether, as John became aware by the Spirit that he was about to hand over to another, he wondered if Jesus would continue his unique ministry of baptism in water. If he did (and we cannot be sure of that, of course), he is not left wondering long. He catches a gleam of divine revelation straight from heaven revealing to him that Jesus will be a Baptiser too, but a Baptiser with a difference. He will immerse His followers not into the cold running waters of Jordan, but into blazing fire!

And did this really happen? Was it merely a figure of speech? Well, step with me into the Upper Room on the day of Pentecost. The message of the gospel is almost complete. Christ had lived and died, had risen again and had ascended to the Father. The facts of the gospel story were all in order. But what was needed now was for those facts to be 'set on fire.'

The disciples sit in the Upper Room like frightened sheep in a pen. Then, suddenly, the Holy Spirit descends and instantly these timid and dispirited disciples are set ablaze. They go out into the streets and, such is the power that accompanies them, they compel the attention of the multitudes and Simon Peter opens the gates of the kingdom to 3,000 souls.

What turned these frightened disciples into men and women who were invincible? It was this: the reigning Christ had reached down from heaven and immersed them in the flame of the Holy Spirit. As I have stated, all the facts of the gospel were complete, but what good are facts unless they are set on fire. It is the fire of God that turns beliefs into blazing convictions. In terms of propagating any message, only as ideas are inflamed do they count for anything.

Now, when it comes to the doctrine of the Holy Spirit, we must accept the fact that opinions vary on this subject. Take the term 'the baptism of the Spirit', for example. Some say that it is what happens at the time of conversion. Others say it is subsequent to conversion. Others claim you can only say you have been baptised in the Spirit if you have spoken in tongues. Now, my question to you is this: whatever you believe about the operation of the Holy Spirit in your life, are you now, at this moment, on fire for God? Have you had an encounter with this Christ of burning, cleansing flame?

How do we know if the fire of God is burning within us? What are the evidences that our lives have been set ablaze by the Spirit of God? One way is to consider the three functions of fire and evaluate our lives by those criteria. The outline I am using is not original to me but I find the three statements it makes concerning the function of fire simple yet wonderfully to the point.

1. FIRE EXTENDS OUTWARDLY

The natural function of fire is to spread. That's why we have fire engines and insurance companies. I remember, on one occasion, travelling from Winnipeg to Brandon in Canada on a Greyhound coach and seeing the prairie on fire. We had to wait for several hours before we could proceed as the flames raced across the prairie, blocking the road. Fire, unless it is carefully controlled as in a boiler or a grate, is never content to remain in one place: its nature is to spread. You can put up a sign that says 'Stop!' or draw a line and forbid it to cross, but it laughs at all boundaries, leaps over all barriers. Fire extends *outwardly*.

Just as it is the natural function of fire to spread, so it is with the fire of the Holy Spirit. If your life has been touched by the divine fire, then, inevitably, the desire to share the gospel and set others on fire with what you have received yourself will have been generated in you.

Let me share with you some lines from T.S. Eliot's famous poem, *The Four Quartets*:

The only hope, or else despair
Lies in the choice of pyre or pyre
To be redeemed from fire by fire
We only live, only suspire
Consumed by either fire or fire.

Consumed by either fire or fire? What does he mean?

There are two fires burning on this earth; we might call them the divine fire and the devilish fire. One is a fire that ravages, the other a fire that redeems. And we must choose to which fire we respond: the fire that blisters or the fire that blesses.

The greatest issue facing the world now, in the twenty-first century, can be expressed in T.S. Eliot's line – either fire or fire. Look at the fires racing across the world at the moment: the fires of moral permissiveness, the fires of militant Islam, the fires of terrorism. Here in the UK we now live in a nation that has more Muslims than Methodists and, the way Buddhism is spreading, the day may come when there are more Buddhists than Baptists. In the hearts of these people a fire is burning

— the fire of a passion to spread the beliefs they believe the world needs to know. Make no mistake about it, there is a fire burning in their hearts. And the only way those fires can be overwhelmed and overpowered is by the fire of the Holy Spirit burning and blazing in the hearts of people who have had an encounter with the fire-baptising Christ.

Consider again those first disciples on the day of Pentecost. They are shut in behind closed doors for fear of the Jews. They are frozen with fear. But Christ plunges them into the fire of the Spirit and instantly all their hesitancy and trepidation melt away and they burst onto the streets, speaking in languages they had never learned. They are like men and women ablaze. Has a similar thing happened to you? Surely you cannot be content with a flickering spiritual experience when you can experience one that engulfs you in flame.

Can I ask you this personal question: are you driven by a passion to share Jesus in some way? Now I don't want to lay a guilt trip on you because you do not consider yourself an evangelist. But you can pray, share, do *something*. Put in a good word for Jesus Christ. 'Evangelism' is a word people shrink from, but it simply means putting in a good word for Jesus. It has been described as one beggar telling another where to find bread. Now you may already be doing this and, if so, that is wonderful.

I met Jesus Christ when I was sixteen years of age, in South Wales. At that time I was a rugby fanatic. I was on fire about rugby, but when I met Jesus Christ and became one of His followers, I transferred the passion I had for rugby to Him and, for the past sixty years, my heart has been on fire with His love and a passion to reach the lost.

I have always loved the story (somewhat apocryphal, I think) of the young man who was in Bible college, not to prepare for the ministry but simply to gain some knowledge of the Scriptures. Every Saturday morning in this college, one of the students would preach for twenty minutes and the other students would analyse the sermon and give it marks for design, content and so on. This particular young man did not want to participate, but the students thought it might be interesting if he did, and so they said to him, 'Next Saturday morning it's your turn.' 'But I am not here to be a preacher,' the young man protested, 'I wouldn't know what to say.' 'Well, have a go anyway,' they said, 'and we will be as gentle with you as possible.'

On the Saturday morning the young man stood in the chapel pulpit with little or no idea what to say, so, rather nervously, he said, 'Do you know what I am going to say?' 'No,' chorused all the students. 'Neither do I,' he said, and sat down. Of course, the students were disappointed but they encouraged him to think about things a little more in preparation for the next Saturday morning. 'Try once more,' they said, 'and we will do all we can to encourage you.'

The next Saturday morning came and the students had agreed amongst themselves that if he said again, 'Do you know what I am going to say?' instead of saying 'No' they would all say 'Yes.' And this is precisely what happened. The student got up and said, 'Do you know what I am going to say?' whereupon the whole class shouted, 'Yes', meaning that they thought he would talk about some aspect of Scripture. His reply was: 'Well, if you all know what I am going to say there is no point in me saying it.' And once again he sat down. The students decided to try one last time to get him to contribute so they said, 'Next Saturday morning we will be here again, ready to listen to what you have to say. Prepare something for us. Try your very best because we would love to hear you speak about the Scriptures.' The student agreed and, in the meantime, the other students got together again and agreed that, if he began again with, 'Do you know what I am going to say?', half of them would say 'Yes' and half would say 'No'.

On the third Saturday morning the student ascended the chapel pulpit and began as usual, 'Do you know what I am going to say?' Half the students said 'Yes' and half said 'No', whereupon the young man said, 'Then those who know tell those who don't.'

Now, I ask you, can you find a better definition of evangelism than that? Isn't that what it's all about? Those who know tell those who don't.

When you get close to the fire-baptising Christ then you can be sure that the fire will spread from Him to you and from you to others, and you will not remain content until you are praying, witnessing and doing everything you can to win the lost to Jesus Christ. And why? Because fire extends outwardly.

2. FIRE ASPIRES UPWARDLY

It is the natural function of fire not only to extend outwardly but also to burn upwards. It has within it an upward tendency. In that respect it is different from water, which rises and falls. The ancient Greeks, who were, as you know, a philosophical people, used to say that water is the element of the earth but fire is of the heavens. Water, they pointed out, always runs downwards and, though it may rise, as from a fountain, it always falls back to earth again. But fire is different: it leaps upwards towards the sky. The only way you can make a fire burn downwards is by using artificial means to regulate it.

To have an encounter with the Christ of burning, cleansing flame is to be set on fire with praise.

Listen to these verses from Charles Wesley's well-known hymn:

Oh Thou who camest from above
The pure celestial fire to impart,

Kindle a flame of sacred love
On the mean altar of my heart.

There let it for Thy glory burn
With inextinguishable blaze,
And trembling to its source return,
In humble prayer and fervent praise.

Or this verse by Horatius Bonar:

Fill Thou my life, O Lord my God
In every part with praise,
That my whole being may proclaim
Thy being and Thy ways.

One of the things that happened in the great Welsh revival of 1904 was that, as men and women were set on fire, the valleys were filled with the praises of God. In the mines the corridors would ring with the sound of hymns and people praising God. In the department stores someone would strike up a hymn and others would join in as they did their shopping. Football matches would often start half an hour late because of the enthusiasm of the crowds to sing hymns together. And, as miners came up from the mines and made their way home, they would sing the great hymns of the faith and would often stop and pray together before they withdrew into their homes to bathe and remove the coal dust from their faces.

It has been said that the Welsh revival of 1904 was a time more of praise than preaching. Often the evangelist Evan Roberts, who was without doubt a man God used powerfully in that revival, would refuse to speak unless a spirit of praise was present. On one occasion, in the little town of Llansamlet in West Wales, he sat with his face buried in his hands for half an hour because the people were reluctant to praise God. After this time a woman rose and said, 'People have come here today to see the man not the Master.' This brought Evan Roberts to his feet and, pale and trembling with emotion, he rebuked the congregation for not putting God first. These were his exact words: 'One might think you came here from the North Pole but if you had passed by Calvary your hearts would be warmer than they are. You have been expecting me to rise for some time but I could not when you have put man before God.'

All this, as you can imagine, brought deep conviction to that congregation, and soon there were tears of repentance and the meeting finished with a great sound of praise filling the church that spread throughout many homes in the town.

Psalm 132:9 says: 'May your priests be clothed with righteousness; may your saints sing for joy.' You can be sure of this: when you have an encounter with the fire-baptising Christ, it will lift your heart in perpetual praise and thanksgiving to God.

3. FIRE CONSUMES INWARDLY

Now you may be saying at this stage, 'Selwyn, all this talk about fire ... are you trying to make us into hot gospel fanatics?' Well, consider this: it is also the natural function of fire to burn inwards. Fire is not content to remain on the rim and rind of things. You cannot restrict its operation to the surface issues. By an inflexible law it will bite like acid to the very core and go on burning until there is nothing left to burn.

I once watched a car showroom in the city of Sheffield catch fire. Dozens of cars were set alight, and I watched as the firemen tried to put the fire out. Cars like Daimlers and Rolls-Royces were burnt up within minutes, their paint peeling and their windows shattering. The fire penetrated right to the heart of the showroom and didn't stop until everything was consumed.

To experience a true encounter with the Christ of burning, cleansing flame is to know a fire that penetrates our moral rottenness, purges the soul and scours the imagination clean. God's fire is not content to burn only outwardly or upwardly but inwardly also.

If you tell me that you have had an encounter with the Christ of burning, cleansing flame and you are indifferent to sin (and there are many ways in which sin may continue in your life), then I will tell you that what you have is a pathetic fiction.

I remember speaking a few years ago at a large men's rally in Vancouver, Canada, organised by a ministry called Promise Keepers. I had been told, prior to the rally, that many men were caught up in Internet pornography and, in my message to them, I called on them to turn their back on such things and allow the heavenly fire that Christ promises to burn it out of them. Before I finished my message, men were running from all parts of the auditorium, one big enough to seat around 10,000 people, and I never did finish that sermon because of the eagerness of those men, several hundred of them, to kneel before God and allow the Holy Spirit to burn the dross out of them.

We are living at a time when standards are not taken as seriously as they should be by Christians. For instance, nowadays, many young Christians see no problem with sleeping together prior to marriage. Christians are suffering from a thing called 'gradualism' whereby we slowly become immune to things that once would have shocked us. How we need God's fire to burn out the moral rottenness in our lives!

The way for a passion to be overcome is by a stronger passion. Our problem is not that our bad passions are too strong but that our good passions are too weak. We are not sufficiently on fire for God.

Listen to another verse from a Charles Wesley hymn:

Refining fire, go through my heart
Illuminate my soul
Scatter thy life through every part
And sanctify the whole.

Someone has pointed out that there are three kinds of fire: stage fire, strange fire and spiritual fire. Stage fire is the kind of fire you see painted on to canvas on a stage. It looks real, but that's all it is: a painted flame.

Strange fire is the fire that we try to light here on earth that relies more on our ideas and enthusiasms than it does on the power and presence of God. There is an account in the Old Testament (in Leviticus 10) where two sons of Aaron were killed because they did not follow the right procedures in relation to the fire upon the altar.

Then there is spiritual fire, the fire that comes from the Christ of burning, cleansing flame.

Is the fire of God burning in your life? Are you one of Christ's incendiaries, spreading His love and passion wherever you go? I invite you now to pray this prayer with me, believing the words of our Saviour who said: 'Ask and it will be given to you; seek and you will find; knock and the door will be opened to you.'

PRAYER

O God, as we watch the various fires burning and racing across the face of the earth, we pray that You will take away our small thoughts and our small love and replace it with a burning passion for Yourself that reflects Your burning love for us. We are sick of our disgusting indifference, our slowness to see how spiritually perilous are the times in which we live. Forgive us, dear Lord, and baptise us afresh with heavenly fire. Give us a Pentecost at any cost. The altar of our hearts is open and ready for You to move in and through us. The offering is laid. Now, Lord, send the fire!

~8~

THE DEBT
COLLECTORS

MATTHEW 18:21-35

Then Peter came to Jesus and asked, 'Lord, how many times shall I forgive my brother when he sins against me? Up to seven times?'

Jesus answered, 'I tell you, not seven times, but seventy-seven times.

'Therefore, the kingdom of heaven is like a king who wanted to settle accounts with his servants. As he began the settlement, a man who owed him ten thousand talents was brought to him. Since he was not able to pay, the master ordered that he and his wife and his children and all that he had be sold to repay the debt.

'The servant fell on his knees before him. "Be patient with me," he begged, "and I will pay back everything." The servant's master took pity on him, cancelled the debt and let him go.

'But when that servant went out, he found one of his fellow-servants who owed him a hundred denarii. He grabbed him and began to choke him. "Pay back what you owe me!" he demanded.

'His fellow-servant fell to his knees and begged him, "Be patient with me, and I will pay you back."

'But he refused. Instead, he went off and had the man thrown into prison until he could pay the debt. When the other servants saw what had happened, they were greatly distressed and went and told their master everything that had happened.

'Then the master called the servant in. "You wicked servant," he said, "I cancelled all that debt of yours because you begged me to. Shouldn't you have had mercy on your fellow-servant just as I had on you?" In anger his master turned him over to the jailers to be tortured, until he should pay back all he owed.

'This is how my heavenly Father will treat each of you unless you forgive your brother from your heart.'

Whenever Jesus Christ wanted to drive home to His disciples some deep spiritual truth, He usually presented it in the form of a story. Jesus was the Master Storyteller – nobody could tell a story like Him.

As a preacher, I have found that people often listen to a sermon from behind a mental barricade – they have got their defences up. They are very fearful about what they are listening to and don't want to be challenged. A story, however, can get in behind your defences and glide into the central citadel of the mind. Then, before you realise it, the truth has been received and your conscience begins to sting with confirmation of the point and you begin to realise that the truth that you were defending against has got in. That is the power of a story!

Jesus was always telling stories, and this one about a servant drove a particular truth into the disciples' hearts. The Amplified Bible says that a servant owed his master ten million dollars. That's a huge sum! All the taxes in Judea, Samaria and the whole of Israel didn't come to a fraction of that amount. So Jesus was using a deliberately exaggerated sum of money for the sake of emphasis. No servant would owe his master ten million dollars.

One day, the master said to all his servants, 'Come on, pay your debts!' They all came to him, including the man who owed him ten million dollars, and the master said, 'You are forgiven. It is cancelled.' Just imagine this happening if you owed someone this enormous sum! You can be sure that when Jesus said a servant owed his master ten million dollars the disciples' ears pricked up. They would have wondered exactly what Jesus was implying, because they knew a situation like that was incredible. Jesus had their attention at this moment. Then He went on, 'The master said to the servant, "I will forgive you. And then, amazingly, the servant went out and found someone who owed him just ten dollars. He said to him, "Come on, pay me what you owe me." And the man who owed him ten dollars said, "I am sorry, I cannot pay". So the servant called the jailers and they thrust the man into prison and into the hands of torturers because he could not pay the money.'

So that was the story Jesus told. The question is, why would a man act in the way the servant did? Why would someone who had been forgiven for amassing a debt of ten million dollars not forgive someone who owed him ten dollars? It doesn't make sense. What was Jesus *really* trying to teach here? Why, having been forgiven such a massive sum, would the servant not have shown generosity, magnanimity and large-heartedness towards someone who owed him a paltry sum?

I wonder if the reason was that, even as he heard the master say 'Now I forgive you', he failed to realise in his heart how much he had been forgiven. You see, it is one thing to know something in your head, but another thing to know it in your heart. The longest journey in the world is from the head to the heart – a mere eighteen inches. Wherever I go in the world I find Christians who have heard the message that they have been forgiven but it has never really reached their hearts.

When people say to me, 'My problem is that I cannot forgive', I say to them, 'That is not your problem. It is that you don't know how much you have been forgiven. If you fully realised how much you have been forgiven by Christ, then you would find it easy to forgive other people.' If you find it difficult to forgive, then I would ask you, 'Do you realise how much you have been forgiven?' When you came to Jesus Christ He forgave you a massive debt. No one else could forgive us, but He came and forgave us our sins.

One of the greatest problems in the Church of Jesus Christ is that people do not have a sense of realised forgiveness. They know it intellectually, but it is 'underneath their hats'. It has never swept through them. Oh, the wonder and joy of being forgiven! That's the greatest thing that can ever happen to you, and without that there will be all kinds of problems in life.

Now, let's consider the amazing climax of Jesus' story: 'This is how my heavenly Father will treat each of you unless you forgive your brother from your heart' (v.35).

I think those are some of the most incredible words in the whole of Scripture. I used to think that what Jesus was saying here was that if you do not forgive your brother from the heart then, when you die, you will go to hell, and there be tortured. But that is not what Jesus is saying. He is making the point that, unless we demonstrate forgiveness to others in the same way that we have received it ourselves, there will be a terrible toll upon our personalities. We will find ourselves incarcerated, in chains, shut off from life, condemned to an inner disruption. It is not in the next life but in this life that we will experience torture.

Let me see if I can expand on this a little bit. You see, when God made this universe He built it according to certain laws. There is the law of gravity, which means that, if I were to drop something right now, it would be pulled to the ground by the force of gravity. Not only has

God built this universe and put great laws in place which govern the stars, planetary systems, plants and so on, but He has also built certain laws into your personality. If you do not obey these laws you will suffer the consequences. If you were to fall from the top of a building to the ground you wouldn't break the law of gravity, you would break yourself. Whenever we violate a principle of Scripture we have to pay the cost. When we break the laws He has built into our personalities a debt builds up and that debt has got to be paid. And the way that debt is paid is extremely important.

What do we say in the Lord's Prayer? 'Forgive us our debts, as we also have forgiven our debtors.' If you break a law and God forgives you, but you are holding resentment and bitterness against someone else, then you have broken a law and within you a debt will arise. Invisible torturers will go to work because, in God's universe, there are no uncollected debts. One of the things that has fascinated me over the years is to see that, when people are holding unforgiveness and bitterness in their hearts, consciously or unconsciously, a debt accumulates within them. That debt piles up and has got to be paid. If you violate that moral law and hold bitterness in your heart, then guilt will descend upon your spirit.

It is interesting to see how people deal with this guilt. Let me explain what I mean. As we harbour unforgiveness we build up a debt within us, and any debt cries out to be paid. Guilt settles upon the soul and, if you hold bitterness or resentment in your heart, then you can be sure that guilt will be there because you are violating a principle of God. God says, 'As you have been forgiven, forgive others.' You say, 'Well, Lord, thank You for forgiving me, but I don't feel like forgiving other people.' Why is this? Because unforgiveness gives us a sense of power over people, and we like to feel powerful. It feels good. But God says, in effect, 'If you hold onto that then let Me tell you what will happen. Guilt will descend upon your spirit and invisible torturers will go to work.' What for? To collect the debt.

Now, I want to tell you the three ways in which that debt can be paid. One way is to *attempt to pay it yourself.* A medical doctor once told me that, with most of the people he sees as patients, 80 per cent of their symptoms may be the involuntary confessions of guilt. This is because if there is guilt within us, within our personalities, it has got to be paid and many of the sicknesses we suffer are a way of paying for our guilt ourselves. We can punish ourselves in the strangest ways. The word 'psychosomatic', applied to medical conditions of this kind, is made up of the Greek words *psyche*, meaning soul, and *soma*, meaning body. What this suggests is that symptoms occur in the body because there is a disturbance in the soul that it finds too much to bear and so transfers to the body. So many of the problems we experience in our bodies are the result of some internal stress, some anxiety, something going on inside us.

When I was a pastor, as I was for eighteen years before I founded CWR, I would go to visit sick people. I wouldn't pray for these people until I had talked to them about what was going on inside them, because I knew that many of the bodily problems we have and the sicknesses we carry are the result of some internal stress. Often the problem would be some unresolved guilt, and I would then deal with it through prayer. Sometimes the person would come to me a few days later and say, 'You know that sickness I had? It has gone, it has disappeared! Did you pray for my healing?' 'No, I didn't pray for your healing,' I would say, 'because I've learned that the problems we carry and the symptoms we show are often the result of some internal problem.'

Now, that doesn't mean that the next time you see somebody sick you say, 'Ah! I know what is wrong with you. You have got some debt inside you. Come on, get down on your knees and repent!' That would be taking what I am saying to extremes, and we must be careful not to do that. But just bear in mind that a *large part* of the physical problems that we experience, though by no means all, are psychosomatic in origin – a view upheld by research done among doctors by the British Medical Association in the United Kingdom. What doctors often have to do is treat the symptoms of an illness because the real problem is inside, and they are trained to deal with the body, not the soul.

I come before you as a doctor of the soul. That's my expertise and that is where I am at home. I don't know much about the body, though I know where my heart is! It is in the middle of my chest, slightly inclined to the left. I know that it pumps blood to the extremities of my body and I know the blood comes back to the lungs, where it is filtered for the oxygen that I breathe, then it goes back around the body again. That's about all I know about the body! But I know a lot about the soul, and I know that if your soul is not experiencing the release and freedom of God's forgiveness then guilt will arise within you and you will try to pay the debt yourself. I have met people who have this sense of guilt, of unrealised forgiveness, and who become ill in an attempt to deal with it.

Some homes are equipped with smoke detectors that go to work as soon as smoke is made and spray water from the ceiling to put out the fire. God has made our souls like that: if there is guilt within us the invisible debt collectors go to work because God doesn't want any uncollected debts in His universe. The guilt has to be dealt with – and we think we can deal with it ourselves through self-punishment.

There is a second way to deal with guilt and that is by *putting the guilt on to somebody else*. Guilt is not a very nice feeling, so we like to spread it around a little, to get rid of it by blaming someone else. I have found with many married couples I have counselled over the years that one partner has something going on inside them for which they want to blame the other person, and that creates a breakdown.

Let me illustrate by telling you about a man and his wife I counselled once because they were having difficulties in their marriage. The woman was one of the finest Christian women that I have ever met in my life, and I knew without any shadow of doubt that the problems were not of her making. So, I took the man aside and I said, 'Look, she says that you fly off the handle at the slightest thing and that you are always blaming her for things. Why are you doing this?' He said, 'Well, she *is* to blame'. 'I know she is a lovely Christian woman', I said, 'and I feel something is going on inside you. Let's talk about it.' And then he told me the following story. He was in the British armed forces, stationed in Hong Kong, and at Christmas time his wife wanted to return home to the United Kingdom to be with the family because they had little children. But the husband was on duty over Christmas and couldn't leave until New Year. So the wife came home on her own. On Christmas morning the husband went to a church service and while he was there he thought how nice it would be if someone invited him home for lunch – but nobody did. And so he walked the streets of Hong Kong, feeling very lonely, and he was approached by a prostitute who invited him to go with her, which he did. He committed adultery. He came home, never confessed it; never dealt with it. And what happened? You know, whenever you violate a law, guilt arises. He was feeling guilty within himself, and because he didn't like the feeling of guilt, he started spreading it around a bit, throwing it here, throwing it there, and his wife especially became the focus of this.

After the husband had told me this story I said to him, 'Can you see what is happening? There is a debt within you that has not been paid. Let's bring this to Jesus. Let's claim forgiveness. Repent of this.' So he did repent and he stood up a transformed man, absolutely renewed. He went back to his marriage and there was no blame or guilt, there was no transference, there was no throwing things onto other people.

Many marriages are torn asunder because of unresolved guilt. This story is an example of the second way we can deal with guilt.

Now, let me tell you about the third way of dealing with guilt, which is *bringing it to the cross of Jesus and letting Him deal with it, not only intellectually but letting His message flow through the whole of your heart.* Isn't it good news that we can do this? This is how God deals with the torturers.

But you have to understand that those who do not fully receive forgiveness are likely to go around with a sense of guilt, and imagined guilt is as destructive as real guilt. So you had better hear the message of Jesus Christ as He says, 'If you do not forgive your brother his trespasses then what will happen is that invisible torturers will come into your heart and torture you because that debt has got to be paid in some way.'

Many years ago, I wrote something in *Every Day with Jesus* on the subject that I am talking about now. It was just 300 words, which is all I can put on a page in *Every Day with Jesus*, but I heard from a reader, a woman who was a doctor, who wrote,

As I read your words I realised that I had been living for years with an unrealised sense of forgiveness. Oh, I understood it intellectually but the message had never really reached my heart and because of this I was striving unconsciously to pay back the debt until my soul screamed out in pain. The torturers were not long in coming and soon the result of my striving was an allergic sickness that incapacitated me. I was on my knees after reading your words, asking the Holy Spirit to help me comprehend the wonder of the fact that I had been forgiven, that my debt had been fully and entirely paid, and He did that in a wonderful way. Praise God, all sense of indebtedness has gone! No longer am I trying to exact payment from myself, no longer need I be driven by a hidden debt that seemed to overwhelm me. I began to realise, for the first time, in all its depth, the meaning of the phrase 'He did it for me'. There is no more debt to drive me in exacting payment from myself. No more debt. My life has gently been turned around and in the last few days I have realised my allergic sickness has gone.

C.S. Lewis said that forgiveness is a wonderful idea until you have someone to forgive! Years ago, in the valleys of Wales, there was a man who had been brought up in a Christian home and taught the principles of the Christian life, but in his teens he walked away from what he had been taught and became a rebel. He swore and blasphemed the name of Christ at every opportunity and his friends would say to him, 'Stop swearing so much and blaspheming the name of Jesus,' but he kept on doing it. Then one night he walked into the church and sat at the back and he heard a preacher talking about Jesus, saying that He could forgive sins. When the preacher finished, that young man came running up the aisle and flung himself to the ground, with tears pouring down his cheeks, and within a few minutes he was wonderfully won to Jesus Christ and he was saved and converted and filled with God's Holy Spirit. And that young man, now many years older, is myself.

After that I used to go to church and at testimony meetings the pastor would say, 'Would anyone like to give a testimony of their experience of Jesus?' I would stand up and say, 'I am forgiven,' and then sit down. The next week the pastor would say, 'Is there anyone with a testimony?' And I would say, 'I am forgiven,' and sit down. And the next week I would do the same. After a few weeks the pastor came to me and said, 'Selwyn, do you think you could say one or two more words?' But that was the one thing I had to say because the wonder of the fact that I am forgiven was the greatest thing in my life. I am free! The message of forgiveness had gone right through my heart: all those debts are cleaned up! I don't have to pay them now. Jesus has paid them for me – on the cross!

Let me tell you one last story. Many of you will know of the Anglican priest, Dr John Stott, who was associated for many years with the church of All Souls, Langham Place, in London. One Sunday, before the church service, some of his workers were out in Harley Street, which is where many psychiatrists have their rooms. A woman had just come out of a psychiatrist's office and was walking down the street, so they gave her an invitation to the church. She went to the church that night and she listened to Dr Stott preaching a simple message of salvation in Christ and, right after it, she went and gave her life to Christ Jesus. She said, 'For a whole year I have been going to a psychiatrist with what I thought was a guilt complex. I have paid him so much money. He talked to me about "transference", explaining that it is what often happens if a person is angry against their parents but unloads it instead onto the psychiatrist. But the only transference I knew anything about was the complete transference of what was in my bank account to his!' She went on, 'He couldn't do anything to get me well because no psychiatrist can deal with real guilt.' The lady came to All Souls, heard the message of salvation and gave her life to Jesus Christ. She said, 'One moment, one moment at the cross, did me more good than one year on a psychiatrist's couch in Harley Street.'

Perhaps you are someone who has never come to Jesus Christ as your Lord and Saviour and has not known the forgiveness of sins. If you are a Christian and you are saying, 'I have found it so difficult to forgive,' then realise that the reason you find it difficult to forgive is because you do not realise how much you have been forgiven. You are like that servant in the story Jesus told. He might have heard his master forgiving him but it had never got into his heart, and so he went out and tried to collect the debt from other people.

Maybe within you there is a load of guilt and you don't know why it is there. God wants to deliver you from that and He wants to forgive you your sins. So, if you have never received the forgiveness of God for your sins, pray this prayer now:

PRAYER
Lord Jesus, I come to You now for forgiveness of my sins. Cleanse me from all unrighteousness and make me whole. Take away the guilt that is within me and make me a new person.

AND FOR THOSE WHO HAVE ALREADY RECEIVED CHRIST
Heavenly Father, I pray that the cleansing blood of Jesus, Your Son, may wash away my sins. O Father, I thank You for the message of forgiveness, I thank You that Jesus came to die upon the cross for our sins. Before, I heard it in my mind, my intellect, but it never spread through my personality to give me a sense of jubilant freedom. I am free from all guilt because Jesus carried it for me on the cross at Calvary. Visit me now by Your Holy Spirit and make me realise that the torturers have gone out of my soul. I don't have to pay the debt myself, I don't have to make others pay. You have paid it all and I receive it and thank You for it, in Jesus' name. Amen.

9
LOVE THAT IS
EXTRAVAGANT

MATTHEW 26:6–13;
JOHN 12:1–8

While Jesus was in Bethany in the home of a man known as Simon the Leper, a woman came to him with an alabaster jar of very expensive perfume, which she poured on his head as he was reclining at the table.

When the disciples saw this, they were indignant. 'Why this waste?' they asked. 'This perfume could have been sold at a high price and the money given to the poor.'

Aware of this, Jesus said to them, 'Why are you bothering this woman? She has done a beautiful thing to me. The poor you will always have with you, but you will not always have me. When she poured this perfume on my body, she did it to prepare me for burial. I tell you the truth, wherever this gospel is preached throughout the world, what she has done will also be told, in memory of her.'

Matt 26:6–13

Six days before the Passover, Jesus arrived at Bethany, where Lazarus lived, whom Jesus had raised from the dead. Here a dinner was given in Jesus' honour. Martha served, while Lazarus was among those reclining at the table with him. Then Mary took about a pint of pure nard, an expensive perfume; she poured it on Jesus' feet and wiped his feet with her hair. And the house was filled with the fragrance of the perfume.

But one of his disciples, Judas Iscariot, who was later to betray him, objected, 'Why wasn't this perfume sold and the money given to the poor? It was worth a year's wages.' He did not say this because he cared about the poor but because he was a thief; as keeper of the money bag, he used to help himself to what was put into it.

'Leave her alone,' Jesus replied. 'It was intended that she should save this perfume for the day of my burial. You will always have the poor among you, but you will not always have me.'

John 12:1–8

Someone has described this incident as the loveliest deed in the Gospels. You may or may not agree with that statement but, whichever way you look at it, it is interesting that it drew from Jesus an unusual commendation.

Picture the scene with me. Jesus is sitting in the house of Simon the Leper. Presumably he was a healed leper as no one in those days would have gone anywhere near a person suffering with that condition. It is just two days before Jesus' crucifixion and He and His disciples are reclining around a table, enjoying rest and refreshment. It was usual for the women to serve the meal and then retire to the kitchen, leaving the men to eat and talk amongst themselves. Against this cultural backdrop we see Mary of Bethany bursting suddenly into the room carrying a vase of expensive perfume and, instead of taking a little and applying it to Jesus' face or hands as might have been expected, she pours the entire contents over Him, drenching Him with the precious liquid. In John's account, she starts to wipe Jesus' feet with her hair. However you look at it, it was an act of great extravagance. It aroused the indignation of some of the disciples, especially Judas who pointed out that the perfume could have been sold and the money given to the poor. Isn't it strange that whenever anyone gives their all to Jesus there are always people around who become defensive, critical and hostile. Extravagance never makes sense to those of a pragmatic mindset – but what offends and challenges them delights the heart of the Lord.

Now Jesus invested this incident with a deathless memorial, predicting that it would be spoken of throughout all time (Matt. 26:13). The Scripture that tells the story has a strange magnetism about it, something compelling and irresistible that demands to be preached, as any preacher will tell you. It conveys something that Jesus wants to highlight and hold up for our consideration. In fact, when I announced that I was about to leave my first church for another one, a little old lady had this to say to me, 'Young man, I have listened to you with great interest in the past but you are not ready to leave this church until you have preached the whole gospel', and pointed out I had not preached on this verse. I preached on it the next Sunday!

If this act of extravagance was commended by Jesus, who dares to say otherwise. To be commended by Jesus is my all-consuming ambition. There have been some ambitions in my life that I frankly confess have been unworthy. In the early days of my ministry I sought the plaudits of my peers: I said and did things with the intention of attracting their praise and attention. I was careful not to offend and I tiptoed through certain issues, drawing back from challenging people when I should have. As I have grown older the emptiness and pointlessness of such ambition has become apparent to me, proving myself has lost its appeal and in its place has come this burning desire to be commended by my Saviour.

I have come to realise that the Christian life is first and foremost about intimacy with Jesus, not about spiritual techniques. We can be orthodox in our doctrine, blameless in our character and efficient in our service but all these things are as ashes upon a rusty altar if we know nothing of a burning, romantic and intimate relationship with the Lord Jesus Christ. Do you know who taught me most what intimacy with the Lord means? It was Mary of Bethany. I have spent a lot of time studying the Bible and it has taught me many things – Greek, Hebrew, systematic theology, hermeneutics, homiletics – many good and important things. But it was Mary, in an intimate moment with the Saviour, who taught me what was most important: not how orthodox is my doctrine (important though that is), but how passionate is my devotion. That's what mattered to Jesus. That's what He commended. That's the picture He memorialised for all time.

If we can understand what brought about this great commendation from Jesus, you and I can put ourselves in the way of receiving it too.

The first thing I want you to understand about Mary's act is this:

IT WAS PROMPTED BY A PERSONAL LOVE FOR JESUS

'She has done a beautiful thing to me,' says Jesus (Matt. 26:10, emphasis mine). She did it not to make an impression, nor, in a subtle way, to draw attention to herself as people sometimes do, but simply out of personal love for Jesus. Jesus saw through that act to the pure and unsullied motive that lay behind it, and commended her for it.

Whenever Mary is seen, she is seen at the feet of Jesus. She sat at His feet, she fell at His feet, she washed His feet with her hair. I suggest that if our eyes are not on Jesus, but rather upon a cause, then we are missing the point. Some people are so caught up in the cause of Christ they forget the Person of Christ. Some even betray the interests of the Lord they serve, as in the case I remember of two of my deacons who actually came to fisticuffs in a disagreement. Christianity *is* Christ.

It is so terribly easy to forget the Person and focus on the cause of Christ, as I know from my own life. The Bible college I went to had this motto, 'Let me never lose the important truth that I must love Thy Self more than Thy service.' Even so, this didn't prevent me one day, early in my ministry, preaching a sermon in which I referred to Pleromatic Humanity, Pleromatic Divinity and Hypostatic Union (all of these terms being ways of explaining the mystery that Christ is both human and divine). At the end of it, a Professor at Swansea University came up to me and said , 'I have to tell you, Selwyn, you are more brilliant than Einstein.' 'Why do you say that?' I asked, trying to look suitably modest. 'Well,' he said, 'it is said that only twelve people understood what Einstein was talking about. With you, I doubt if there is even one. If I am not mistaken,' he went on, 'Jesus said, "feed my sheep", not "feed my giraffes!"' I got the message, loud and clear! I realised with shame that I was preaching way above people's heads because I was more interested in preaching to impress than in the One I was preaching about.

We can and should work for Him, but what He really wants is our love. He uses our talents and abilities but what He wants more than anything is our love. So I urge you to forget the cause and focus on the Person. Again I say, Christianity *is* Christ.

> But I know whom I have believed,
> and am persuaded that He is able
> to keep that which I've committed
> unto Him against that day.

These are words from a wonderful old hymn by Daniel W. Whittle which my grandmother used to sing, especially when she knew she was dying. As senility and illness overtook her she forgot the words, but she would just keep repeating the word 'Him'. The Bible is all about Him. All truths converge on Him. He is hub of the evangel, the heart of the gospel. It's all about Him. We can study the Bible as an interesting book all about principles and ethics and moral codes, or we can come to it as the place to see the luminous figure of Jesus.

Something that saddens me greatly is that people tend to think of their Quiet Time of Bible study and prayer as a means to spiritual growth. Of course it is, but this view places the emphasis on us. 'It's not about me', as a popular worship song reminds us, 'it's all about You, Jesus.'

Activity and intimacy are not, in fact, mutually exclusive. The point is that our activity for Christ should grow out of our intimacy with Him. Worship first, work second. That is the most efficient way to serve Him and we are more likely to earn His commendation when everything we do is out of love for Him.

One day, years ago, while I was staying with a family, they asked the daughter of the house to say grace. She said, 'Lord Jesus, I love You more than anything else in the whole world.' I burst into tears. Could anything be more delightful to the heart of our Lord than that?

IT WAS A GIFT GIVEN AT A TREMENDOUS COST
What was the cost of Mary's gift? It cost her everything she had. We understand from Scripture that the cost of the vase of perfume was about 300 denarii, which was equivalent to a year's wages. We are not just talking about extravagance here, but super-extravagance. Without hesitation she broke the vase and poured what was, perhaps, the present-day equivalent of a gallon of Chanel No. 5 over His head. Note that it wasn't placed carefully but poured liberally, lavishly, extravagantly, soaking Jesus from head to toe, and then she wiped His feet with her hair.

So let me ask you what serving Jesus costs you, in terms of time, commitment and so on. Does it hurt for you to give? Is there the stain of blood upon it?

Scripture tells, in 2 Samuel 24:18–25, of the altar King David wanted to build to the Lord on the threshing-floor of Araunah the Jebusite. David had made a serious mistake to which God responded by sending a plague upon the people and David wanted to make an atoning sacrifice to stop this plague. Araunah was willing for David to take the threshing-floor without payment but David declared, 'No, I insist on paying you for it. I will not sacrifice to the LORD my God burnt offerings that cost me nothing' (v.24).

I was reading recently about the construction of the cathedrals of Britain, many of which were constructed against the wishes of those who disapproved of extravagance. Many lives were spent, and lost, in the dangerous course of their construction. The comment of the author was, 'It gave to them the glory of costliness.'

I knew something of this when I was asked by the Lord to give away the first hundred pounds I had ever saved. There was a need I knew I could meet, but I struggled to give it away. When I did, the release it gave me was tremendous.

The Welsh Revival began when a young girl who was shy, retiring and inhibited by nature stood up and said, 'I love the Lord Jesus Christ with all my heart!' The effect of this was dramatic and far-reaching. I told that story on a particular occasion in a rather fashionable church, and a woman who was also very inhibited and introverted and would never dream of raising her hands in public prayer, walked down to the front and began to worship the Lord in this way. The minister looked at her as if she had gone mad. Soon others began to raise their hands and he didn't know what to do. Afterwards, the deacons met to consider the matter and decided that their worship was too rigid. It ended up that the minister was baptised in the Spirit. So, sometimes it is not money but our inhibitions that we need to give to the Lord.

THE TIMELINESS OF THE DEED

'She did it to prepare me for burial' (Matt 26:12; John 12:7). What on earth did Jesus mean by that? I wonder whether Mary had some gleam of revelation that Jesus was on His way to His death. I think she sensed from His countenance, perhaps the look in His eyes, that He was on His way to die. With an amazing sense of timing, she intuited that if she didn't do it then, she might not have another opportunity. When Jesus died a few days later the women came with precious spices and ointment to anoint the body of Jesus ... but He wasn't there. They missed the opportunity, while Mary sensed that this might be her only chance to honour Him. She ministered to Him by taking advantage of the moment. That's why Jesus commended her.

In our lives too there are times when extravagance is appropriate. For instance, I would love to see abandoned the Spartan philosophy, the tendency to go for the lowest bid, which sometimes prevails in evangelical circles and produces only mediocrity. I often wonder sadly why so many of the places where God is represented have to be so frugal and ordinary in their furnishings? Is it necessary to omit works of art? Must we live under self-imposed restraint and guilt for fear of being accused of neglecting the poor? Of course there should be no careless flaunting, but there are times when we, like Mary, need to break a vase and pour it all over Jesus.

Mary was liberated out of herself into an act of dramatic devotion. Throwing caution to the wind she was lifted above arithmetic calculation to abandoned compassion. She had her focus right and she did not allow her reserve to keep her from acting in the moment that might never come again. 'A certain excessiveness is an important ingredient of greatness,' says Lloyd Ogilvie in a book entitled *Life Without Limits*. I like that thought.

I draw the lesson from this that Jesus is not someone who simply wants a relationship with me but that He wants a relationship that is intimate and passionate. Often we are willing to have a relationship but we don't want it to be too passionate. In the Upper Room Jesus said to His disciples, 'Whoever has my commands and obeys them, he is the one who loves me. He who loves me will be loved by my Father, and I too will love him and show myself to him' (John 14:21). In the context of a committed relationship Jesus promises to reveal Himself to us. Often we want the disclosure without the relationship, but Jesus is not indiscriminately intimate.

'I tell you the truth, wherever this gospel is preached throughout the world, what she has done will also be told, in memory of her.'

Matt. 26:13

Why, we must ask, does Jesus invest this story with a deathless memorial? Why does He hold it up for all time? The reason Jesus said the story of Mary and the outpoured perfume would be told everywhere for all time, I believe, is because He wants to keep drawing our attention to the fact that the most important thing in our lives is not our grasp of doctrine, important though that is, but how passionate we are in our love for Him.

The scribes and Pharisees were of all people the most highly educated in the Scriptures at that time. They believed God's Word and taught many of the right things, priding themselves on their strict adherence to the Old Testament Law, and yet Jesus did not prop any pictures of them on His mantelshelf, so to speak. The picture dear to Jesus, the one He held close to His heart, the one that brought a tear to His eye and a smile to His face as He moved towards the cross, was that of Mary. Because, I reiterate, what touches Jesus' heart is not so much what we know but how much we love. What really matters is not how pure we are but how passionate. The scribes and Pharisees were fighting over theology but Mary was kneeling at His feet. And that to Him was beautiful.

We like to brag about our children or grandchildren or great-grandchildren by showing pictures of them, and our Lord appears to do this. Like a proud father He takes out His wallet and says, 'Do you want to see something beautiful? Do you want to see the delight of my life? Take a look!' That's why this story of Mary has its place in the Word of God. And He said, '... wherever this gospel is preached ... what she has done will be told ...' That is why we are considering it now. As far as we know, Mary never did very much: she didn't cast out demons like the disciples, she never worked miracles. All she did was to love the Saviour and it was the way she loved Him that made the difference: she loved Him passionately, extravagantly, lavishly.

See the picture once again: extravagant love flowing with its wonderful aroma not only from the veined alabaster vase in her hands, but also from the vase of her heart, a heart broken against the hard reality of her Saviour's imminent death. She sensed that something was going to happen to the Master and she wanted in some way to minister to Him in His hour of need. She broke that vase and the perfume has lingered behind the ears of every century and its scent lingers to this very day. Perhaps the fragrance of that perfume, as it flowed down from Jesus' head down over His garments, clung to Christ all through the humiliation of His trials, the indignity of His mockings, the pain of His beatings, the inhumanity of His crucifixion, mixing with the heavy smell of sweat and blood. The air must have caught a hint of fragrance from His garments until, shamefully, they were stripped from Him and gambled away. And maybe, just maybe, it was that scent, amid the stench of the rabble gathered around the cross, that gave the Saviour strength to say, 'Father, forgive them for they know not what they do.' As Mary walked away from the cross, that same scent probably still lingered in the hair, now limp, that she had used to dry the Saviour's feet, a reminder of the love that spilled from His broken body on the cross. It was the perfume of a sacrifice that would rise to heaven and bring pleasure to the nostrils of God: so pure, so lovely, so truly extravagant. It was a vase He never regretted breaking ... Neither, I am sure, did she regret the vase she had broken.

Are you ready to commit yourself to Jesus, to make Him the centre of your life, to be more focused on Him than on His cause, to see that what He wants is not just your work but your worship, not just your service but your love? Are you willing to spend more time with Him in prayer, even if it is only fifteen minutes of each day? It will be costly, but the rewards are so much greater than the cost.

As the Spirit draws near to your heart, remind yourself that you may not feel like this again. Take advantage of this moment to offer Him every unyielded thing, to break the vase and become extravagant with your love.

How much will it cost you to abandon your inhibited approach, to be extravagant and say, 'Lord, I love you!' Mary's gift was costly because it cost her reputation also. You too have costly gifts that will bring pleasure to His heart. There may be many things you hold and that hold you that you need to break away from in order to be His and His alone.

Sometimes we have to be fools for Christ, to give Him our lives in one great prodigal act of joy and blessing.

I remember some years ago I took my wife to Hawaii and, as we sat on the beach, I heard a man talking to some young people about surfing. I am always on the lookout for good sermon illustrations, so I pricked up my ears. 'It's wonderful to ride the waves,' he told them, 'but wait, be patient, and you will see one wave that will rise above the others. Out there where the big waves are there's what they call the white water. Time your trip. Then, when the big wave comes, don't fight it. Lean into it! Go with it!'

This is what we have to do: live like surfers in the place of the white water, riding the waves with God, waiting for the big one. When it comes, we won't just ride it, we will lean into it, go all the way with it.

If Mary had not been impulsive she would not have broken the vase. Had they not followed their impulses, the four men would not have torn off the roof to let down their paralysed friend at the feet of Jesus. The lesson is this: what we want to keep for ourselves we lose. If we forget ourselves, let go, we gain immortality. This truth has kept the event alive for two thousand years.

The Christian faith is filled with moments of burning extravagance when sensing the timing of God is the most important thing. I look back at those points in my life when I have sensed that God was calling me to a moment of extravagant love, times when, stepping out in faith, I have been able to say 'yes' to God's dares. There have been other times when, because of fear and cowardice, I have failed to give of myself, when I have put safety first rather than Saviour first. I wonder how far I might have been swept had I been able to lean into the wave and go with it.

There are people who plan their lives carefully and meticulously. You know how it goes: they plan to have a nice little house in a nice little area with, perhaps, a nice little boy and a nice little girl, with a nice little retirement plan so that they can be nice and safe and secure in the days ahead, and then, at the end of it all, a nice little place in a nice little cemetery with a nice little name neatly engraved upon the headstone. If that is all that happens in your life and you know nothing of those moments of extravagant devotion when you step outside yourself and break the vase of devotion, then all you will have accomplished is to pamper yourself into mediocrity when you could have forgotten yourself into immortality.

~ 10 ~
THE DIVINE EQUATION

~

JOHN 20:21

'As the Father has sent me, so I send you.' (NLT)

This is a statement of tremendous importance. Like many of the famous utterances of Christ it is seemingly simple yet positively staggering in its implications.

If you look carefully you will see that it is framed in the form of an equation: As ... so. 'As the Father has sent me so [or in the same way] I send you.' With these words the Son of God set out a sum on the spiritual blackboard of the disciples' souls that must have left them somewhat bewildered. They had scarcely recovered from the shock of His crucifixion when He placed upon them a tremendous responsibility.

Picture the scene with me. The disciples are huddled together in the Upper Room like frightened sheep in a pen, when suddenly the risen Jesus comes and stands amongst them. It is almost time for His departure to the royal throne in heaven, but before He returns He has something He wants to say that puzzles and confuses the disciples. So, confronting them, He utters these riveting words, making it crystal clear that He is returning to heaven and turning over to them the task He commenced on earth. His earthly ministry is coming to an end and they are to extend His ministry. The responsibility of perpetuating the divine plan is now being transferred into their hands.

Think of it! Here was the Son of God passing over to a few frightened disciples the greatest task ever committed to men. Consider for a moment a chief executive handing over a multinational company to an office boy! The disciples had little to commend them, naturally; they were not men of learning, they had no official status and no financial backing. Yet these facts do not seem to deter the Son of God. Looking them straight in the eyes He says, in effect, that He is about to send them in the same way that the Father had sent Him. That was a breathtaking statement. No wonder He had to breathe on them and energise their flagging spirits with the power of the Holy Spirit!

The spiritual sum Jesus set out for His disciples is what I call the Divine Equation. Let me bring it into closer focus for you.

If we can grasp something of what it meant for Christ to come to this world, if we can understand more of *His* side of the equation, then we will be able to understand what it meant for His disciples then and what it means for us, His twenty-first-century disciples.

In thinking this matter through I have been greatly helped by reading a book about New Testament patterns of ministry by a man called Colin Cruise. In it he traces the compass points in the ministry of Jesus and then looks to see how they relate to the life and ministry of the apostle Paul. Three things, according to Cruise, are evident in the lives of both Christ and Paul: they both had a clear sense of being sent, they both experienced a wonderful empowerment of the Holy Spirit and they were both conscious that they were sent to serve.

Let us consider first this fact that Jesus knew He was sent, that He carried with Him, wherever He went, a sense that He had been sent by the Father to this earth to accomplish a task.

'He who receives you receives me, and he who receives me receives the one who sent me.'

Matt. 10:40

'The Spirit of the Lord is on me, because he has anointed me to preach good news to the poor. He has sent me to proclaim freedom for the prisoners and recovery of sight for the blind, to release the oppressed, to proclaim the year of the Lord's favour.' (Luke 4:18–19)

'My food,' said Jesus, 'is to do the will of him who sent me and to finish his work.'

John 4:34

The Gospels are filled with references or statements that clearly show Jesus knew He had been sent, that He had a mission.

What does it mean to carry a sense of being sent? For Jesus it meant He knew that God had called Him to a task. For Him there was no identity crisis, that frightening experience that comes upon you when you don't know who you are. It is apparent from the Gospels that right from His earliest days Jesus knew what He was doing in the world. The cross cast its shadow over all of His life, even as He worked at His carpenter's bench, and intimations of it were seen early in His ministry. God the Father broke in from His cloudy pulpit to make it crystal clear what was going to happen and where He was being sent. Similarly, Jesus spelled it out clearly for His disciples, to whom He presented His 'manifesto' in the Sermon on the Mount. It was this manifesto that put Him finally on the cross. Those who would follow Him must be willing to face danger, privation, difficulty, effort, toil, exhaustion, the shedding of blood, sweat and tears. They were required – as He requires us today – to sacrifice, to give up things, to meet a cross. There was a cross for Him and there is a cross for us, and it must be faced if we are to come alive with power and with glory. The way leads to Calvary and He sends His disciples along it in the same way: with clear instructions.

Knowing who we are and what we are about is the starting point for all that we do. I shall never forget a particular moment in my life when I was in Dublin at the invitation of a friend, Billy Gibbons, who ministered in the Church of Ireland. He was an enthusiastic reader of *Every Day with Jesus* and had been to several seminars I had conducted. I had got to know him very well. This is how he introduced me to his church: 'Now let me tell you about Selwyn,' he said. 'He is not a scholar. His knowledge of Hebrew and Greek is basic. I know that because I have talked to him about it.' (I did not, as it happens, have the privilege of gaining a degree: I studied for three years at a college which, at that time, did not offer degree courses and we were taught by good men who were spiritually competent but not academically inclined.)

'Selwyn is not a psychologist,' Billy went on. 'He has studied psychology and I guess he knows more about how the human personality functions than some psychologists but, in the true sense of the word, he is not a psychologist. I don't doubt that if he had wanted to become one, he could have done it.' I was grateful for that! At that point I was praying that he would stop because I was thinking, 'These people are *really* going to be interested in listening to me after this.' But he continued: 'Selwyn is not a theologian. He understands theology very well, but again he is not, in the strictest sense of the word, a theologian. Let me tell you what he is: he is a telegram boy who brings us messages from God. He identifies the wrong road down which we are travelling and calls us back to the old paths. He has the ability to touch the spirit, not just the mind.' And then he said – and this is the bit that staggered me– 'I want to say before you all this morning that I would give up all my degrees, all my scholarship, all my experience, for one tenth of his ability to touch the heart and make us realise we have heard from God!'

I sat there feeling mixed emotions. You see, I fancied myself as a bit of a theologian, a bit of a psychologist, a bit of a scholar! But suddenly I was stripped of any illusions. Much later I had time to think all this through and I came to see that it is only when you are emptied of your illusions that you can know your real self, the self that can be sent, what you should be doing and what you should not be doing. I realised that you have to understand what you are not before you can understand who you are. We are not here to peddle the gospel; we are here to glorify God. It means saying no to the good in order to say yes to the best.

That experience helped to clarify things for me in the most wonderful way. I went through the gamut of emotions: from apprehension, fear, a little anger, to a sense of being overwhelmed. Suddenly I knew who I was: a telegram boy delivering messages from God. I have had no illusions since that day. Whenever I stand to speak before an audience, or sit down to write, I am engaged on that task to which I have been sent.

I will never forget being called to the ministry. I was working in a Welsh coal mine at the time, actually underground, when I heard a voice, not audible but thundering nevertheless in my soul, and it was clear and strong. It was the Lord saying, 'I want you in the ministry.' That was a wonderful moment. Had I not been able to recall it I would have quit the ministry a few months after I came into it, when I was struggling with the task. But God sent a man, Brother Goldsworthy, to encourage me. He was a veteran Christian, not actually a member of the church of which I was the pastor, but someone who attended services regularly. He told me that God had given him a word for me (the same verse, in fact, that was given to me on the night of my conversion), Jeremiah 33:3: 'Call to Me, and I will answer you, and show you great and mighty things, which you do not know' (NKJV). God had also given him a little glimpse into my future. I would not always be a pastor, he said, but after the Lord had taught me certain lessons I needed to learn in this role, He would guide me into a ministry far beyond anything I could imagine 'Keep calling on Him, keep close to Him in prayer and step by step He will reveal to you His deep purposes for your life.' How amazingly true his prophetic words proved to be.

Years before, as a schoolboy, I heard my headmaster say, 'Hughes has written the best essay I have ever read.' He also said, on another occasion, 'You might make a good rugby player.' Two things were heard. One reverberated within me in a way the other didn't. Why was that? Because, I believe, I had heard something about that gift of writing before – in my mother's womb.

The starting point for all of us is to know who we are, and what we are doing here. Our identity is that we are beloved of God, chosen to play a specific part in His programme. We need to be comfortable with that. Jesus knew that He had come from God and that He was going to God. You and I too come from God. There needs to be a sense of 'sentness' in us all, an understanding of why we came into the world. This enables us to carry on when our sense of who we are becomes disproportionate. Sometimes God dislocates people before He relocates them, just as I was stripped of all pretension in order to know who I was. Sometimes God takes away from people what they enjoy doing or being, as He did with Abraham. Jesus Himself was dislocated and then relocated. The disciples were dislocated from their sense of themselves as fishermen, tax gatherers and relocated as disciples on a mission. Dr W.E. Sangster, a famous Methodist preacher of former times and one of my heroes, said that sometimes the only thing you have left, after the stripping away, is the sense of being sent.

Sometimes God sends us directly to perform a task, as He did in my case. We are called by His grace and then we are given a purpose, a task to do for Him. In being sent we are given opportunities to express different gifts, and everyone is gifted to do certain things well. At other times, the sending is in being put by God in a particular place where we meet a need.

This sense of 'sentness' arises out of three convictions: knowing who we are, knowing that we are loved and knowing where we are going. It requires us to be wholly available for God, willing for Him to send us wherever He wants us to go. Our response must be that of the prophet Isaiah: 'Here am I. Send me!' (Isa. 6:8). Some are sent and remain in the same place for years, others are continually sent to different places. The sense of being sent can hold us whenever we feel discouraged in our task as we remind ourselves that we were chosen and sent to do it. I have come to know that a telegram boy is all I am. Let me warn you that if you think too much of your importance then God will burst the bubble of applause!

Creating a Mission Statement is generally a helpful exercise. I worked out my own Mission Statement years ago and it came down to this: *I am sent to help people with their problems.* There is an inward compulsion for the task.

We come now to consider the second similarity in the lives of Christ and Paul: the empowerment of the Spirit. This is the wonderful gift of God which is given along with the responsibility of the task.

Did the Father leave Jesus to execute the task for which He was sent in His own strength? No. Heaven opened after His baptism in the Jordan and the Spirit descended upon Him. This was a special and particular anointing of the Spirit, a supernatural clothing for a special task. But before beginning His ministry Jesus was sent into the wilderness for forty days and was there tempted by the devil. It was a further empowerment because it is under test that the Holy Spirit makes us powerful. Jesus was tempted by the devil to use His power to feed Himself, to take risks with it and to bypass the cross. Let me say that we cannot make too much of the cross. It is the means by which God saves the people of the world. But what we need most of all in this world is a mighty empowerment of the Holy Spirit.

Predicting His death, Jesus uttered these words: 'Now my heart is troubled, and what shall I say? "Father, save me from this hour,"? No, it was for this very reason I came to this hour' (John 12:27). It was by the Spirit's power He was able to accomplish His mission.

In order to accomplish their mission, the Spirit's power was given to the disciples of Jesus. After His death and resurrection, Jesus came to His disciples, cowering behind locked doors, and breathed on them, saying 'Receive the Holy Spirit' (John 20:22). Some say it was the regeneration power of the Spirit that He breathed on them. Others say that this was a rehearsal for Pentecost, perhaps to give them a taste of what was to come. It was a wonderful event, certainly, but it seems that it didn't make much of an impression on them. Fifty days later they received the full empowerment of the Holy Spirit as He descended on each of them in tongues of flame (Acts 2) and everything was different after that. The Spirit makes the difference.

And what do we see in the life of Paul? Clearly he had a sense throughout his ministry of working with divine energy. Some believe it was the energy of Christ. This acknowledgement of divine power at work in him, enabling him to overcome all opposition and obstacles in the pursuance of his ministry, is something to which he refers time and time again in his letters. Honestly admitting his natural weakness he told the Corinthians who were scorning him: 'Therefore I will boast all the more gladly about my weaknesses, so that Christ's power may rest on me' (2 Cor. 12:9).

Paul spoke of God's power continually and in different ways: 'his eternal power' (Rom. 1:20), 'this all-surpassing power' (2 Cor. 4:7), 'his incomparably great power' (Eph. 1:19). Moreover, he understood that he, Paul, had been equipped for all God sent him to do through the empowerment of the Holy Spirit, and his prayer for the Ephesians was that they too might be strengthened with this power 'through his Spirit in your inner being' (Eph. 3:16).

I will never forget the experience of the Spirit that came to me some time after I was converted. I thought that, in giving my life to Christ, I had it all. But, as Dr Martyn Lloyd-Jones was wont to ask of people, I had to ask myself: 'For heaven's sake, why are you as you are?' There was indeed more to come!

Finally, let us consider the third similarity between Christ and Paul: their consciousness that they were sent to serve.

First of all, let us consider Jesus. The thread of servanthood is woven through His life and it was this lesson, above all others, He chose to focus on with His disciples on the night before His passion. A dispute had broken out amongst them as to who was the greatest, which draws a sharp reproof from Jesus:

> 'The kings of the Gentiles lord it over them; and those who exercise authority over them call themselves Benefactors. But you are not to be like that. Instead, the greatest among you should be like the youngest, and the one who rules like the one who serves. For who is greater, the one who is at the table or the one who serves? Is it not the one who is at the table? *But I am among you as one who serves.*'
>
> Luke 22:25–27, my emphasis

Having first demonstrated His identity as one who serves by washing their feet He went on to say:

'Now that I, your Lord and Teacher, have washed your feet, you also should wash one another's feet. I have set you an example that you should do as I have done for you. I tell you the truth, no servant is greater than his master, nor is a messenger greater than the one who sent him. Now that you know these things, you will be blessed if you do them.' (John 13:14–17)

Turning now to the apostle Paul, it is clear to us from the book of Acts and his letters to the early Christian communities, that Paul always had a high sense of serving. He begins his famous letter to the Christians in Rome with the words 'Paul, a servant of Christ Jesus, called to be an apostle and set apart for the gospel of God ...'

To the Corinthians he wrote, addressing divisions in the church: 'What, after all, is Apollos? And what is Paul? Only servants, through whom you came to believe ...' (1 Cor. 3:5).

He exhorted the Colossians not to be moved from the hope held out in the gospel 'of which I, Paul, have become a servant' (Col. 1:23).

Not only was He willing to serve, he seemed always to be asking the Lord, 'How can I serve You better?'

So too, in letter after letter, he encouraged others to see their lives in terms of service to the Lord:

For the kingdom of God is not a matter of eating and drinking, but of righteousness, peace and joy in the Holy Spirit, because anyone who serves Christ in this way is pleasing to God and approved by men. (Rom. 14:17–18)

You, my brothers, were called to be free. But do not use your freedom to indulge the sinful nature; rather, serve one another in love. (Gal. 5:13)

Serve wholeheartedly, as if you were serving the Lord, not men, because you know that the Lord will reward everyone for whatever good he does, whether he is slave or free. (Eph. 6:7)

When I started in my first church, someone said to me, 'I wonder when you will make your first mistake.' Take note, not when you will make a mistake but when you will make your *first* mistake. I did it as soon as I arrived! I came into the ministry with the thought, I am ashamed to say, 'All these people are here to serve me.' I had to appropriate for myself the truth that the one who is greatest is the one who serves the most.

Service is the thing, and there are questions we must ask ourselves. 'How do we serve Jesus? What is service and where is the service done? 'How can we serve people better?' My good friend in America, Dr Tolbert Moore, a pastor with a significant ministry, keeps a nail, a bowl and a towel on his desk. One day I asked him about it and he replied, 'I keep them there to remind me of the need to serve.'

Paradoxically, we cannot serve until we have been served. We have to kneel at the feet of the Man who washed the feet of His disciples and let Him wash our feet. That's where I am. Life is all about service and my service is to serve many thousands of people a day with the Bread of Life. All I do is to draw attention to the Word and say to them, 'Have you ever thought of this?' This is the task to which God sent me. As He transferred the task He transferred the power also.

Let's look again at the Divine Equation posed by John 20:21. Jesus has done what He was sent to do. Now God is sending you to accomplish a task. Your part is to know who you are and what you have been sent for, to take upon yourself the attitude of a servant and to open yourself up to receive the empowering of the Holy Spirit. Let no one think that God is expecting more of you than you are capable of giving. By His mighty power He did it through Jesus, He did it through Paul, He did it through me. He will do it through you also.

11

THE
FOUR ANCHORS

ACTS 27:27–29

On the fourteenth night we were still being driven across the Adriatic Sea, when about midnight the sailors sensed they were approaching land. They took soundings and found that the water was one hundred and twenty feet deep. A short time later they took soundings again and found it was ninety feet deep. Fearing they would be dashed against the rocks, they dropped four anchors from the stern and prayed for daylight.

The apostle Paul is a prisoner on a ship sailing for Rome, where he intends to appeal to Caesar against the unfair charges levelled against him. The ship became a plaything in the hands of a hurricane called the 'north-easter'. Day after day the ship is driven across the Adriatic Sea by the great storm. In panic the sailors jettison the cargo allowing the boat to run freely, but the storm continues to rage and, after two weeks, they are giving up all hope of being saved. Suddenly, in the middle of the night some of the sailors realise that they are heading for the rocks and one cries out in terror, 'Breakers ahead!' Soundings are taken and, realising that they are approaching land, they let down four anchors that hold the ship steady.

Storms in the Adriatic were so powerful that many ships had more than one anchor. This vessel had four and, in darkness and great peril, they were held fast by these four strong anchors until daylight came and the storm subsided. Reading on we learn that though the ship was lost, all 276 souls were saved.

Like Paul aboard this ship, we all go through storms in our lives. I have certainly been through a few in my time and some of them have been very rough, such as when my wife and then both my sons died, the time when I almost lost my faith and a period when I thought my life's work was over. There have been church storms and personal storms and the question has been put to me, 'What has held you through life's storms?' Reflecting upon this, I came to see that there have been four anchors I have learned to drop, four convictions that have sustained me in the crossing currents and in the most severe of storms. These four convictions, which I liken to anchors, have shaped my life and saved me from spiritual shipwreck. I want to pass them on to you and my hope and prayer are that they will be a source of assurance for you too.

ANCHOR ONE: THERE IS A GOD WHO LIVES

This is my unshakeable belief, notwithstanding the philosopher Nietzsche and some theologians of the 1960s who have claimed that God is dead. They saw the universe as a kind of clock created by God which is now winding down. God, they said, was once in control, as He seemed to be in biblical times, but no longer. The universe is unravelling. As God has not shown Himself in power since the days when Jesus was on earth, the conclusion is that He is dead. This kind of thinking gives rise to the sort of joke made by the comedian Woody Allen: 'If God's there He could at least cough or make my Uncle Sasha pay the bill in a restaurant.' How tragic!

Some will allow that God is not dead but claim that He is absent from His universe, not involved in it. This is what is called Deism.

Then there are those who say the world began by itself. I remember a bit of humorous doggerel from many years ago which goes something like this:

'There is no God!' the speaker cried,
'Don't let your thoughts be chained.
The universe evolved itself, the world itself contained.'
Just then an urchin in the crowd
A skilful pebble throws
Which landed very accurately on his atheistic nose
'Who threw that stone?' the speaker roared,
At which the cockney elf, intuitively keen, retorts,
'No one, mate – it frew itself.'

The Bible says a lot about the fact that God is alive. Paul, in Acts 17, told the Athenians that, 'The God who made the world and everything in it is the Lord of heaven and earth and does not live in temples ... he himself gives all men life and breath and everything else ... [and] he is not far from each one of us. For in him we live and move and have our being' (vv.24–25,27–28).

The writer to the Hebrews says, 'The Son is the radiance of God's glory and the exact representation of his being, sustaining all things by his powerful word' (1:3).

This means that, if He were to withdraw His hand from us, we would not live. We depend on Him but He depends on no one. He lives in the power of an endless life. The Communists boasted that they would topple every king from his throne here on earth and then they would topple the king from the skies. But the writer to the Hebrews exults in the words, 'Your throne, O God, will last for ever and ever ...' (1:8).

Some might say, 'But these are just words. How do you know God is still alive now? What practical proof do you have?' To which I can only reply that I know because of His involvement in my life, the fact that I talk to Him and He talks to me, constantly.

I remember a discussion one time when I was a student in Bible college in Bristol about when God was at His best. Some thought at the time of creation. Others thought it was at the time of the deliverance from Egypt, or the incarnation, or the cross, the resurrection, or perhaps the descent of the Spirit at Pentecost. In my opinion God was at His best in 1944 when He showed up in a little mission hall tucked away in the Welsh valleys, and saved my soul. He took a young, wilful and rebellious young man, gave him the gift of eternal life and called him to the ministry. That young man was me.

God put His life in me and I stand with C.S. Lewis who wrote, during World War II, 'If by some strange circumstance I saw a bomb coming toward me and I knew there was no way of escape, I hope I would be able to say, "Poof! You are just a bomb. I'm going to live forever. The life of God is in me and nothing can turn it away."'

I feel sorry for people who do not believe in God. God is there and He is my friend. I have a relationship with Him that is wonderful and I talk to Him every day. Once, on a plane journey, I got into conversation with a man who told me he didn't believe in God. 'Tell me about the God you don't believe in,' I said, and when he'd told me I said, 'I don't believe in Him either.' I was then able to talk to him about the God I do believe in.

ANCHOR TWO: THERE IS A GOD WHO LOVES
The greatest thing about God is not that He is eternal or that He is omnipotent. These things are wonderful, but the greatest thing about God is the fact that He is love. Let's be clear about this. I'm not saying that He is lovely or loving, but that He is love. The distinction is important. Take love out of an angel and what do you get? A devil. Take love out of a human being and what do have? A sinner. Take love out of God (as if you

could) and you have nothing! God is love and this means that everything God does is according to LOVE.

How amazing it is that this great God of ours loves. He loves you! He loves me! Nothing in us gave rise to it, nothing in us can extinguish it. Do you realise that God loves you? When did you first realise this? I am not talking about the realisation that you are saved, but the realisation that you are loved by God. I didn't always have a concept of a God who is love. The concept of God I once carried in my heart was of a God who is harsh, vindictive, cold, austere. Now I have come to know that He is nothing but love and that He loves me. The love of God is the theme of the Bible. The love of God is the greatest theme of the universe. The love of God is powerful.

I've had more than one person tell me that their problem is they don't love God enough. But that is not their – or our – problem. The problem is that we don't know how much He loves us. The realisation of this love is powerful. But so many human beings have no awareness of this. They are so damaged that they can't feel it. It is just a word for them and it never gets into their hearts.

I know that God loves me and His love is without measure. I am accepted in the Beloved. He loves me not for what I can do but because ... He is love. There is no reason behind it. He loves me as I am but, at the same time, He loves me too much to let me stay as I am. When we realise how much we are loved, the scales fall from our eyes and our own love flames in response. At times I have spoken to people about God's love and they have begun crying. Thundering sermons commanding them to do this and do that fail to have this effect, but the realisation that we are loved personally conquers our hearts, dispels our antipathy and overwhelms all our suspicion and distrust. What makes *Les Misérables* and other musicals so appealing? They tell the story of *love*, and we are all longing to be loved. The amazing thing is that we are loved – by the world's greatest Lover!

But then comes the inevitable question: If God is love, why does He allow tragedies to happen? Why does He not intervene to prevent them?

If we think about life's evils we realise they are the product of human ignorance, stupidity, carelessness and sin thwarting the good desires of God for this world. They are a consequence of God's gift of free will, without which we would be puppets not people. So, to my mind, to ask why God allows such things to happen is a shallow question. The deeper question is: Why did God create human beings but not subject them to His control?

In our world, power and control are merged: in God's world they are separate. His power is not control. He created us free agents, made to love, serve, influence and help one another. By the same token we have the ability to hurt one another. We could not have the blessing without the risk, and God took the risk. Sin entered the world bringing with it sorrow and suffering, vulnerability to the folly and crimes of others. But would we rather live in a world in which this could not happen? Would we wish God to have made us creatures unable to influence each other for good, to be friends, to guide, comfort and help each other. Unable to love? It would surely be a hateful and unendurable existence, loathsome to us all.

Rather than make us puppets, God in creation gave a divine salute to freedom. Freedom is the highest value, and this includes freedom to make a mess of things. God gave us freedom and we misuse it, but God allows only what He can use because He is committed to bringing good out of evil. Now we see the wrong side of the tapestry with all its roughness and tangled threads, its seeming confusion, but one day we will see the eternal tapestry from the right side, in all its beauty.

God's love is the second anchor I drop – the love of a God who loves us too much to abolish our freedom. The terrible tragedies that occur serve as a wake-up call to the world and also to the Church, alerting God's people to the needs of the world. They pave the way for revival and sober God's people, providing windows of opportunity. God is with us in these tragedies, hurting, seeking to turn tragedy to triumph, loss to gain. He does not cause them but works creatively through them. He has to stand back because He respects our human freedom too much to exert His control.

There's an old hymn by Priscilla J. Owens we used to sing which is not so often heard nowadays:

Will your anchor hold in the storms of life,
When the clouds unfold their wings of strife?
When the strong tides lift and the cables strain,
Will your anchor drift, or firm remain?

We have an anchor that keeps the soul
Steadfast and sure while the billows roll,
Fastened to the Rock which cannot move,
Grounded firm and deep in the Saviour's love.

ANCHOR THREE: THERE IS A GOD WHO LISTENS
Between people there is frequently a communication breakdown. Recently, I overheard one woman in a supermarket queue ask another, 'Is it Tuesday or Wednesday today?' To which she replied, 'I don't know, dear, I'm not from around these parts.'

And so it is with many people, as you will have discovered! They are not actually listening but simply waiting to have their turn at talking.

But perhaps some don't listen because they have never been listened to, as I have often been told by those I have counselled. Listening is the most powerful way of showing someone you care and so, in training our counsellors at CWR, we put much emphasis on teaching them to listen.

When it comes to talking to God, I am totally confident, on the basis of numerous scriptures, that He always listens. We have His full attention and He both hears and answers our prayers. Prayer is powerful and we should be praying frequently. But people often tell me that they have given up on praying 'because God doesn't listen'. That does not accord with God's Word, but undoubtedly the matter of God's response can be problematic for people. I am reminded of the woman who told me she had prayed for God to give her love for her husband, and He didn't, so she took this as guidance to seek a divorce from him. This was a dangerous and tragic misunderstanding.

God gives us this assurance:

... if my people, who are called by my name, will humble themselves and pray and seek my face and turn from their wicked ways, then will I hear from heaven and will forgive their sin and will heal their land.

2 Chron. 7:14

But we are not to expect that He will always answers our prayers in the way we want them answered. His answer may be 'Yes', 'No', 'Not yet' or, as I have personally experienced, 'I will give you something better'. I know that God listens to me when I talk to Him, and I know this doesn't mean He is going to do everything I ask. I leave the judgment to Him and thank Him for all my answered prayers, no matter what His responses have been.

Long ago, when I was a little boy, my pastor used to pray that God would make me a preacher. He used to tell me this and it disturbed me because, at that time, I didn't want to be a preacher. He would put his hand on my head and say, 'You are going to be a preacher one day.' My mother told me I used to push it off because that was the last thing I wanted to be – film star, perhaps, or a doctor, but not a preacher. But then I met Jesus and all my life has been an answer to prayer, a testimony to the power of prayer. There is no doubt that God listened to my pastor.

God hears and answers: 'Call to me and I will answer you and tell you great and unsearchable things you do not know' (Jer. 33:3).

ANCHOR FOUR: THERE IS A GOD WHO LEADS

There is an old saying that when we talk to God that is prayer and when He talks to us that is schizophrenia!

God has led me through many situations, some of them difficult, where I have asked Him, 'Why am I here? What am I doing here?' At such times all I knew was the certainty of His leading.

From personal experience I have come to know that there is a God who leads and guides, just as long, long ago He led Abraham from Ur of the Chaldeans to the promised land. God led me as a young man to leave Wales and, in due course, to establish a church in London. At a certain time in my life I was preparing to settle in America. A group of church elders had told me, 'We will build you a home, pay for your furniture and provide a church. Go ahead!' It seemed like a marvellous opportunity but God said, 'No.' So I returned to London to face a future that was, in many ways, uncertain.

One day a man who was about to board a plane in Tokyo was led by God to reroute his journey in order to come to London to deliver a message to me. These were his words to me, 'God has told me the things that you are planning in your heart. He wants you to go ahead.' So I did, with two young children and no money in the bank, not knowing at all how it was going to work out. Out of that came the London Revival Crusade and eventually Crusade for World Revival (CWR).

God led me into writing *Every Day with Jesus*, which I have been writing for over forty years, and one day I had the inexpressible joy of having a woman come up to me and say, 'You saved my life. I was about to commit suicide but you were there, through *Every Day with Jesus*.' And this is only one of the many times people have told me something wonderful came about in their lives through something God led me to write.

I have spoken of some remarkable instances of God's leading but there's another way in which He leads us. Robinson Crusoe said, 'How wonderfully we are delivered when we know nothing of it.' This is what is called 'unconscious guidance' and I think this is the greatest thing. At times like this we find ourselves in a quandary, we doubt and hesitate, not knowing whether to go this way or that, and then there comes a strange impression on our mind that causes us to move in a particular direction. With this kind of guidance we don't know we are being led until we look back and see our life as if it were a mountain trail, and then we see the operation of God's hand as we consider each step we took and each one we might have taken but did not.

Nothing is too trivial for divine omnipotence: He guides us in the smallest things of life. His eye is upon you and upon me as upon the tiny sparrows, not one of which, Scripture tells us, will fall to the ground apart from the will of the Father (Matt. 10:29).

My ultimate goal in my ministry is to bring people a little nearer to God, and He has led me in accomplishing this purpose. Once, during an interview, I was asked how I accounted for my success, having come from a humble home in a small mining village in Wales. I was not born to greatness. My parents didn't have much, but they had character and integrity. They paid their bills and sometimes went without themselves in order to be able to provide for me. They took good care of me throughout my upbringing and they prayed that God would lead me into His purposes for my life.

So let me identify again the four anchors that have held me fast through the storms of life: *God lives, God loves, God listens, God leads*.

Into this reassuring and encouraging revelation we drop our anchors. What more do you need to enable you to sail through life or to hold you steady when the storms come?

National Distributors

UK: (and countries not listed below)
CWR, Waverley Abbey House, Waverley Lane, Farnham, Surrey GU9 8EP.
Tel: (01252) 784700 Outside UK (+44) 1252 784700

AUSTRALIA: CMC Australasia, PO Box 519, Belmont, Victoria 3216.
Tel: (03) 5241 3288 Fax: (03) 5241 3290

CANADA: Cook Communications Ministries, PO Box 98, 55 Woodslee Avenue, Paris, Ontario N3L 3E5.
Tel: 1800 263 2664

GHANA: Challenge Enterprises of Ghana, PO Box 5723, Accra.
Tel: (021) 222437/223249 Fax: (021) 226227

HONG KONG: Cross Communications Ltd, 1/F, 562A Nathan Road, Kowloon.
Tel: 2780 1188 Fax: 2770 6229

INDIA: Crystal Communications, 10-3-18/4/1, East Marredpalli, Secunderabad – 500026,
Andhra Pradesh.
Tel/Fax: (040) 27737145

KENYA: Keswick Books and Gifts Ltd, PO Box 10242, Nairobi.
Tel: (02) 331692/226047 Fax: (02) 728557

MALAYSIA: Salvation Book Centre (M) Sdn Bhd, 23 Jalan SS 2/64, 47300 Petaling Jaya, Selangor.
Tel: (03) 78766411/78766797 Fax: (03) 78757066/78756360

NEW ZEALAND: CMC Australasia, PO Box 36015, Lower Hutt.
Tel: 0800 449 408 Fax: 0800 449 049

NIGERIA: FBFM, Helen Baugh House, 96 St Finbarr's College Road, Akoka, Lagos.
Tel: (01) 7747429/4700218/825775/827264

PHILIPPINES: OMF Literature Inc, 776 Boni Avenue, Mandaluyong City.
Tel: (02) 531 2183 Fax: (02) 531 1960

SINGAPORE: Armour Publishing Pte Ltd, Block 203A Henderson Road,
11–06 Henderson Industrial Park, Singapore 159546.
Tel: 6 276 9976 Fax: 6 276 7564

SOUTH AFRICA: Struik Christian Books, 80 MacKenzie Street, PO Box 1144, Cape Town 8000.
Tel: (021) 462 4360 Fax: (021) 461 3612

SRI LANKA: Christombu Publications (Pvt) Ltd., Bartleet House, 65 Braybrooke Place,
Colombo 2. Tel: (9411) 2421073/2447665

TANZANIA: CLC Christian Book Centre, PO Box 1384, Mkwepu Street, Dar es Salaam.
Tel/Fax: (022) 2119439

USA: Cook Communications Ministries, PO Box 98, 55 Woodslee Avenue, Paris, Ontario N3L 3E5, Canada.
Tel: 1800 263 2664

ZIMBABWE: Word of Life Books (Pvt) Ltd, Christian Media Centre, 8 Aberdeen Road, Avondale,
PO Box A480 Avondale, Harare.
Tel: (04) 333355 or 091301188

For email addresses, visit the CWR website: www.cwr.org.uk
CWR is a registered charity – Number 294387
CWR is a limited company registered in England – Registration Number 1990308

Spoken from the Heart
Selwyn Hughes

The first volume of *Spoken from the Heart* contains 12 powerful
sermons and talks delivered by Selwyn Hughes which have blessed
and inspired audiences around the world. This collection has been left
more or less as preached so as to retain the authenticity. It comes with
a CD of Selwyn preaching 'He's Just a Carpenter'.

ISBN-13: 978-1-85345-376-2
ISBN-10: 1-85345-376-5
£8.99

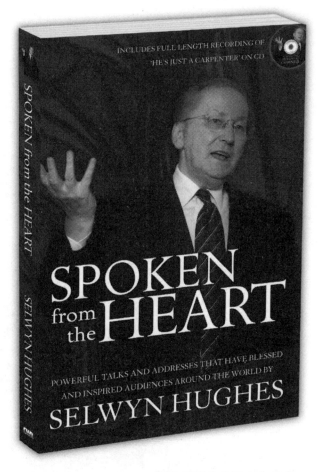

Price correct at time of printing

My Story
Selwyn Hughes

Published just 18 months before his death, Selwyn Hughes traces his
story from his roots in Wales through his conversion and call to the
ministry, to his experiences as a pastor and pioneer in the fields of
Christian counselling in training. It takes in the growth of CWR
from foundation to international organisation. An inspirational
and faith-building book.

ISBN-13: 978-1-85345-296-3
ISBN-10: 1-85345-296-3
£9.99

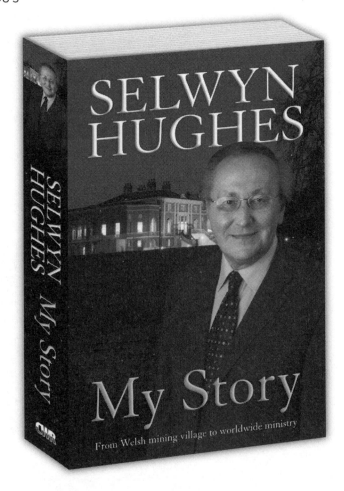

Every Day with Jesus
Pocket Devotionals
Selwyn Hughes

These two latest volumes in the popular series, are beautifully presented devotionals containing thoughts for the whole year from Selwyn Hughes. Designed to help you grow in your relationship with Jesus and enhance your spiritual journey, these pocket-sized books make ideal travelling companions or welcome gifts.

Walking in Faith
ISBN-13: 978-1-85345-399-1
ISBN-10: 1-85345-399-4
£7.99

Joy for Today
ISBN-13: 978-1-85345-398-4
ISBN-10: 1-85345-398-6
£7.99